AF303870

Marx Abbott Hardy Machiavelli Cooper Emerson Joyce
Defoe Melville Montaigne Chesterton Austen Grimm
Stoker Carroll Christie Haggard Hugo
Wilde Maupassant Byron Eliot
Garnett Engels Molière Schiller
Goethe Fitzgerald Hawthorne Smith Kafka
Baum Cotton Einstein Dostoyevsky Hall
Henry Kipling Doyle Willis
Leslie Dumas Flaubert Nietzsche
Stockton Turgenev Balzac Crane
Burroughs Vatsyayana Verne
Curtis Tocqueville Gogol Vinci
Homer Widger Tolstoy Busch
Darwin Whitman Scott
Potter Freud Thoreau Twain Plato Harte
Kant Zola Lawrence Dickens
Jowett Stevenson Burton Hesse
Andersen Cervantes
London Descartes Voltaire
Poe Aristotle Wells Cooke
Hale James Hastings Irving
Bunner Shakespeare
Richter Chambers
Doré da Chekhov Benedict Alcott
Dante Shaw Pushkin
Swift Wodehouse Newton

 tredition®

tredition was established in 2006 by Sandra Latusseck and Soenke Schulz. Based in Hamburg, Germany, tredition offers publishing solutions to authors and publishing houses, combined with world-wide distribution of printed and digital book content. tredition is uniquely positioned to enable authors and publishing houses to create books on their own terms and without conventional manu-facturing risks.

For more information please visit: www.tredition.com

TREDITION CLASSICS

This book is part of the TREDITION CLASSICS series. The creators of this series are united by passion for literature and driven by the intention of making all public domain books available in printed format again - worldwide. Most TREDITION CLASSICS titles have been out of print and off the bookstore shelves for decades. At tredition we believe that a great book never goes out of style and that its value is eternal. Several mostly non-profit literature projects provide content to tredition. To support their good work, tredition donates a portion of the proceeds from each sold copy. As a reader of a TREDITION CLASSICS book, you support our mission to save many of the amazing works of world literature from oblivion. See all available books at www.tredition.com.

Project Gutenberg

The content for this book has been graciously provided by Project Gutenberg. Project Gutenberg is a non-profit organization founded by Michael Hart in 1971 at the University of Illinois. The mission of Project Gutenberg is simple: To encourage the creation and distribution of eBooks. Project Gutenberg is the first and largest collection of public domain eBooks.

Thoughts on Missions

Sheldon Dibble

Imprint

This book is part of TREDITION CLASSICS

Author: Sheldon Dibble
Cover design: Buchgut, Berlin – Germany

Publisher: tredition GmbH, Hamburg - Germany
ISBN: 978-3-8472-1605-6

www.tredition.com
www.tredition.de

Copyright:
The content of this book is sourced from the public domain.

The intention of the TREDITION CLASSICS series is to make world literature in the public domain available in printed format. Literary enthusiasts and organizations, such as Project Gutenberg, worldwide have scanned and digitally edited the original texts. tredition has subsequently formatted and redesigned the content into a modern reading layout. Therefore, we cannot guarantee the exact reproduction of the original format of a particular historic edition. Please also note that no modifications have been made to the spelling, therefore it may differ from the orthography used today.

THOUGHTS ON MISSIONS.

BY THE LATE

REV. SHELDON DIBBLE,

MISSIONARY IN THE SANDWICH ISLANDS.

Go ye into all the world, and preach the Gospel to every creature. — Mark 16:15.
Go — teach all nations. — Matt. 28:19.
Prove all things — hold fast that which is good. — 1 Thes. 5:21.
PUBLISHED BY THE
AMERICAN TRACT SOCIETY,

150 NASSAU-STREET, NEW-YORK.

INTRODUCTORY LETTER.

To my Classmates in Theology.

Dear Brethren in Christ:—Few periods of our lives can be called to mind with so much ease and distinctness, as the years which we spent together in theological studies. The events of that short season, and the sentiments we then indulged, are clothed with a freshness and interest which the lapse of time cannot efface.

Among the questions that occupied our thoughts, no one perhaps was so absorbing, or attended with such deep and anxious feeling, as that which respected the field of labor to which each should devote his life. And many of us then, I remember, made a mutual engagement, that if spared and permitted for years to labor in different portions of the vineyard of the Lord, we would communicate to each other our *mature* views in regard to the claims of different fields.

Thirteen years have elapsed; and I propose to fulfil my engagement, by expressing, in the form of the present little volume, the views which I now entertain in regard to the claims of foreign lands. [Pg 8] To you, my beloved classmates, the book is specially addressed; and if I use a frankness and freedom, which might possibly be construed into presumption, if I were addressing strangers and elder brethren, I am sure that I shall fall under no such imputation when communicating my thoughts to you. I wish to express my thoughts familiarly, as we used to do to each other, and at the same time with the earnestness and solemnity which one ought always to feel when pleading for the perishing heathen.

A free, full, and earnest discussion of such sentiments as those contained in this book, had no small influence, under God, in preparing the way for that extensive work of grace at these islands, which has been denominated the Great Revival. At the General meetings of the mission in the month of May of 1836 and 1837, the main doctrines of this volume were thoroughly canvassed, and with deep effect upon every member present. Our feelings were enlisted, our hearts were warmed, and our thoughts were absorbed by the great topic of the world's conversion. The theme, in all its amazing import and solemn aspects, was allowed to take possession of our souls. It gave importunity to prayer, earnestness and unction to our conversation and sermons, and zeal, energy, and perseverance to every department of our work; and the result was soon apparent in the wide-spread and glorious revival.

It can almost be said, therefore, that the main [Pg 9] sentiments of this volume have received the impress of the Divine approbation.

In the fall of 1837, I was constrained by family afflictions and the failure of my own health, to embark for the United States. As I began to breathe the bracing air of Cape Horn, my strength in a measure revived, and having no other employment on board ship, I sketched the outlines of most of the chapters of this little volume. My heart was full of the theme in the discussion of which I had taken part before my embarkation, and I penned my thoughts freely, amidst the tossings of the ship and the care of two motherless children.

On my arrival in the United States, I revised and filled up the outlines I had sketched, and delivered them, in connection with various historical lectures, at several places, as Providence gave me opportunity. Now, having returned to these islands, I have thought best to give the chapters a second revision, to dedicate the whole to you, and with the help of the press to send you each a copy, accompanying it with my prayers and my most affectionate salutations. And may I not expect, beloved classmates, that you will read the book with candor, weigh well its arguments, admit its entreaties to your hearts, as those of your former associate, and act in accordance with the convictions of duty?

Among the considerations that have prompted me to the train of thought contained in this book, as well as to the views interwoven in my history of [Pg 10] the Sandwich Islands, I may mention, as not the least weighty and prominent, a dutiful respect and filial obedience to the instructions delivered to me, in connection with others, by the wise and devoted Evarts, on the eve of our embarkation for the foreign field. The delivery of those instructions was his last effort of the kind, and they may therefore be regarded as the parental accents of his departing spirit. On that occasion of interest, to which memory can never be treacherous, a part of the charge to us was in the following words:

"From the very commencement of your missionary life, cultivate a spirit of enterprise. Without such a spirit, nothing great will be achieved in any human pursuit; and this is an age of enterprise, to a remarkable and unprecedented extent. In manufactures, in the mechanic arts, in agriculture, in education, in the science of government, men are awake and active; their minds are all on the alert; their ingenuity is tasked; and they are making improvements with the greatest zeal. Shall not the same enterprise be seen in moral and religious things? Shall not missionaries, especially, aim at making discoveries and improvements in the noblest of all practical sciences—that of applying the means which God has provided, for the moral renovation of the world?

"There are many problems yet to be solved before it can be said, that the best mode of administering [Pg 11] missionary concerns has been discovered. What degree of expense shall be incurred in the support of missionary families, so as to secure the greatest possible efficiency with a given amount of money; how to dispose of the children of missionaries, in a manner most grateful to their parents, and most creditable to the cause; in what proportion to spend money and time upon the education of the heathen, as a distinct thing from preaching the Gospel; how far the press should be employed; by what means the attention of the heathen can be best gained at the beginning; how their wayward practices and habits can be best restrained and corrected; how the intercourse between missionaries and the Christian world can be conducted in the best manner, so as to secure the highest responsibility, and the most entire confidence; and how the suitable proportion between ministers of the Gospel retained at home, and missionaries sent abroad, is to be fixed in practice, as well as in principle: all these things present questions yet to be solved. There is room for boundless enterprise, therefore, in the great missionary field, which is the world."

I have not attempted to discuss all the topics here named, but have endeavored to cultivate in some degree, as enjoined in the paragraph, a spirit of *enterprising inquiry.*

If this book shall impart any light on the interesting topic of Christian duty to the heathen, and [Pg 12] be owned by the Saviour, in the great day, as having contributed, though but in a small degree, towards that glorious consummation of which the prophets speak, and to which we all look forward, I shall be richly rewarded.

Your affectionate classmate,
SHELDON DIBBLE.

Lahainaluna, *Feb. 17, 1844.*

[Pg 13]

THOUGHTS ON MISSIONS.

CHAPTER I.

THE TRUE SPIRIT OF MISSIONS.

The apostles, under the guidance of the Holy Spirit, uniformly enforce their exhortations by tender appeals to the example, sufferings, and death of their ascended Lord. Is humility inculcated? the argument is, Christ "humbled himself and became obedient unto death, even the death of the cross." Is purity of life enjoined? the plea is, Christ "gave himself for us, that he might redeem us from all iniquity, and purify unto himself a peculiar people." Is liberality required? we are pointed to Christ, who, "though he was rich, yet for our sakes became poor, that we through his poverty might be rich." Is entire consecration to Christ enjoined? the appeal is, "he died for all, that they who live should not [Pg 14] henceforth live unto themselves, but unto him who died for them and rose again."

In like manner, in gaining a true idea of the spirit of missions, the proper course evidently is, to look at once at the missionary character of the Lord Jesus Christ. He was indeed a missionary. He came to save the lost. He was a missionary to *us*. He came to save *us*.

We had wandered and were lost. We were guilty and condemned. We were in a state of despair. Nothing within the compass of human means could avail in the least to avert the impending wrath of God. All wisdom became foolishness. All resource was futile. Not a ray of hope remained—not the least flickering gleam. Whichever way the eye turned, there was darkness—horror—despair. But Christ came, and hope again visited the earth. It was when we were helpless—hopeless—justly exposed to the horrors and agonies of the world of woe, that Jesus undertook his mission, and appeared for our relief.

This truth cannot be too deeply impressed upon us, here, at the very threshold of our inquiries in regard to the spirit of missions; and to spread it out distinctly before our minds, let us take a simple illustration. [Pg 15]

You are a captive in a foreign land, and have long been immured in a deep, damp, and gloomy dungeon. Sorrow, sighing, and tears have been your meat day and night. Anguish, gloom, and a fearful looking for of death, combined with hunger, cold, and a bed of straw, have induced disease, wasted your flesh, destroyed every energy, and entirely drank up your spirits. Sentence of death is pronounced against you, and the day fixed for your execution. The massive walls and iron grating look down sternly upon you, and rebuke at once all hope of escape. Entreaties, tears, and the offer of gold and silver have been tried, but in vain. Effort and means have given place to horror and despair. The prospect before you is the scaffold, the block, a yawning grave, and a dread eternity. In this extremity a friend appears, and offers to be substituted in your place. The offer is accepted. You, pale, emaciated, and horror-stricken, are brought from your dungeon to behold once more the light of day. The irons are knocked off from your hands and feet—your tattered garments exchanged for cleanly apparel—and a ship is in readiness to convey you to the land of your birth and the bosom [Pg 16] of your friends. The vital current of your soul, so long chilled and wasted, now flows again with warmth and vigor; your eyes are lighted up, and tears of joy burst forth like a flood. But, in the midst of your joy, you are told of your deliverer. You turn, and behold! the irons that were upon you are fastened upon him—he is clothed in your tattered garments—is about to be led to your gloomy dungeon—lie on your bed of straw, and thence to be taken in your stead to the scaffold or the block. You throw yourself at his feet, and entreat him to desist; but when you find his purpose fixed, you finally wish you had a thousand hearts to feel the gratitude you owe, and ten thousand tongues to give it utterance.

The Lord Jesus Christ has done for us all this, and unspeakably *more*. We were under condemnation. The sentence of God's righteous law was against us. The flaming sword of Divine vengeance was unsheathed. All above and around us were the dark frowns of the Almighty and the red lightnings of his wrath. Beneath us was not merely a damp dungeon, but the bottomless pit yawning to receive us, and its flames ascending to envelope our guilty souls. There was no escape. [Pg 17] The prospect was weeping, wailing, and gnashing of teeth—the agony of Jehovah's frown forever. In this extremity the Saviour appeared—substituted himself in our stead—bare our sins in his own body on the tree—received upon his own agonized soul what was our due, and thus delivered us from the untold horrors of eternal death, and opened before us the gate of heaven.

To save the lost, then, was the spirit of Christ. The apostles imbibed this spirit. *It is the spirit of missions.* The heathen are in a lost condition. If we have the spirit of Christ we shall do what we can to save them. The spirit of missions is not something different from, or superadded to, the Christian spirit, but is simply, essentially, and emphatically *the* spirit of Christ. It is compassion for the perishing; and such compassion as leads the possessor to put forth strenuous efforts, and to undergo, if need be, the severest sufferings.

As we shall look somewhat in detail at the manifestations of the spirit of Christ, we shall see very evidently the great outlines of what alone is worthy to be called the true spirit of missions.

Look at the *condescension* of Christ, and learn a lesson of duty [Pg 18] towards the destitute and degraded of our race. The Son of God, by whom were all things created that are in heaven and that are in earth, whether they be thrones or dominions, principalities or powers; who upholdeth all things by the word of his power; before whom ten thousand times ten thousand and thousands of thousands prostrate themselves, ascribing power, and riches, and wisdom, and strength, and honor, and glory, and blessing; of whom it is said, "Every knee shall bow to him, of things in heaven, and things in earth, and things under the earth"—the King eternal, immortal, invisible, the only wise God: this Infinite Being empties himself of his glory, and comes down to toil, suffer and die—and for whom? For us worms of the dust, insects that are crushed before the moth.

If the Saviour had come to our relief, clothed with the glory of heaven and surrounded by his holy angels, even that would have been a stoop of amazing condescension. But look at the babe of Bethlehem, born in a stable, and cradled in a manger; follow him to Egypt, and then back to Nazareth. What humility, [Pg 19] lowliness, and condescension! Look at the Saviour in his public ministry. You find him oftenest among the *poor*, and always so demeaning himself as to be the one that was "meek and lowly in heart." His chosen walk was such, that it could be said with emphasis, "to the poor the Gospel is preached."

Such was the spirit of Christ and such his condescension! Such was the spirit of the apostles. They took much notice of the poor, and charged Paul and Barnabas, when going forth on their mission, especially to remember them. What else, I ask, is a missionary spirit, but to be willing to labor with self-denial and perseverance to elevate and save the low and the vile? Natural men, in the pride of their hearts, are inclined to look down upon the wretched — to regard them with that kind of loathing and disgust which disinclines them to make sacrifices in their behalf. This dislike is such that I have often thought it to be a favor to the heathen, that they are far off and out of sight; for if they were near and directly around many professed Christians, with all their defilement and ugliness in full view, much of the apparent sympathy for them which now exists, would be [Pg 20] turned into contempt and cold neglect. But if such had been the superficial and ill-founded character of Christ's compassion, where should we have been at this present hour? There is not a wretch now wallowing in the deepest mire of sin, who is so vile and low in our eyes, as we all were in the eyes of infinite purity. Yet the more wretched we were, the more deeply did Christ feel for us. *This spirit of Christ is the only true spirit of missions* — the only spirit that will make self-denying, continued, and persevering efforts to save the heathen.

There is no romance in the practical and every-day duties of a missionary. The work is of a humble form, and emphatically *toilsome*. There is but little true missionary spirit in the world. It is not the sympathy of an hour, nor an enthusiasm awakened by romance, but the pure love of Christ in the soul, constraining the possessor to pray earnestly, and to labor cheerfully without notice or applause, for the lowest human objects; and which finds a rich and sufficient reward for a life of toil in leading one ignorant slave, one degraded outcast, or one vile heathen, to accept the offers of salvation. My observation [Pg 21] in the field for thirteen years testifies to the fact, that no sympathy or enthusiasm will come down to the arduous details of missionary work, and persevere in it for years, that does not flow from such genuine and permanent love as our Saviour manifested when here upon earth. The more we become like Christ, the more shall we possess of the true missionary character.

How slow we are to make *real sacrifices* for the good of others! It was not so with Christ. He chose, for our good, to become a man of sorrows and acquainted with grief—to be rejected, despised and hated—to become a mark for the bitterest rage and the finger of scorn.

Go to the garden of Gethsemane. There behold, what even the pencil of the angel Gabriel cannot fully portray. There, in the stillness of the night, the Saviour retires to give vent to the bursting emotions of his soul. Deep sorrow, keen anguish, and excruciating agony roll in, like continuous surges, upon his tender spirit. His strength fails. Low he lies on the cold earth, and the drops from his pale and agonized features, like the clammy sweat of death—no, "like drops of blood"—fall to the ground. [Pg 22]

But the agony of his spirit does not perturb the submission of his soul, nor shake the steadfastness of his purpose. The furious mob arrive, and he calmly yields himself to their disposal. See him in the judgment-hall—meek under insults, forgiving under buffetings and abuse, submissive and quiet under the agonizing scourge. Then behold him, as faint from his gashes and his pains, and sinking under a heavy cross, he slowly moves towards Calvary. Look on, if your eyes can bear the sight. The rough spikes are driven through his feet and his hands—the cross is erected—the Lord of glory hangs between two thieves:—there, his torn, bleeding, writhing and excruciated body is to wear out its vitality in protracted agony. But all this suffering was as a drop in his cup of anguish. O the deep—fathomless, untold agony of his soul, when under the hidings of his Father's face he exclaimed, "My God, my God, why hast thou forsaken me!"

All this suffering and agony the Infinite Son of God endured, that we might be saved. He had a vivid and perfect view of all this, and yet voluntarily assumed it that we might live. [Pg 23]

In view of such an example, what shall we say? If the Lord of glory shrunk not from ignominy and scorn, untold agony, exquisite torture and the most cruel death, can any one possess much of his spirit, and yet consider it too much to forego some of the comforts and delights of this fleeting life, and to labor and toil with persever-ance and self-denial on a foreign shore, to instruct the destitute and the dying—to enlighten the millions and hundreds of millions of heathen, who have never heard the precious name of Jesus, and are entirely ignorant of the consolations of his grace? Is it too much, even to expose one's self to an early grave in a sultry clime, if neces-sary, that some ray of hope may break in upon the gloom of the benighted and perishing nations? God be praised, that the prospect of death did not daunt the spirit of the self-denying Jesus!

O, how has a feeling of shame and deep humiliation come over my spirit, as I have heard the objection, that "Missionaries and mis-sionaries' wives especially go forth to die!" Thanks to the continued grace of God, that some of this spirit of Jesus—the self-sacrificing spirit, the spirit of devotement, even unto death—still exists on earth. Let the objector [Pg 24] inquire seriously, whether much of it reigns in his own bosom; and whether in proportion as he is desti-tute of it, he be not lacking not only in the spirit of missions, but in the spirit of Christ, without which it is impossible to be a disciple. For it is true not only of missionaries, but equally of all Christians, that they are not their own—that they are bought with a price; and are under obligations of *entire consecration*, each in his appropriate sphere, that are as high as heaven and as affecting as the scenes of Gethsemane and Calvary. And we are bound, equally with the early disciples, to count it not only a duty, but "all joy" to labor, suffer and die, if necessary, for Christ's sake, and in the good work which he has given us to do.

Did we become sensible of our lost condition? Did we with one accord lift up our penitent and broken-hearted cries to the God of mercy, that he would provide a way for our salvation? Did the an-gels intercede in our behalf that the Saviour would come? No: *self-moved* he appeared for our relief. He beheld us wedded to our sinful courses; unwilling to be taken from the pit into which we had plunged ourselves, and clinging with [Pg 25] unyielding grasp to the very instruments of our ruin—strangely enamored with the very vampires that were preying upon our souls. The more disinclined we were to sue for mercy, the more the Saviour pitied us; for our very unwillingness to supplicate showed the depth of our ruin.

In like manner, the more indisposed any heathen nation may be to receive us to their shores, admit the light of the Gospel and partake of its blessings, the more deeply should we feel for them, and the more zealously labor for their salvation. That a nation has not called for our aid, but is resolutely determined to keep us at a distance, is a strong argument for being deeply interested in their behalf. Their very blindness and maniac disposition should call forth the deep commiseration of our souls. Such was the spirit of Christ. Such is the true spirit of missions. It is but a small measure of compassion to aid those who supplicate our assistance. The very blindness, guilt, madness and vile degradation of a people, should be to us a sufficient voice of entreaty. They were so to the heart of the precious Saviour, or he never would have undertaken the work of our redemption. [Pg 26] O, when shall it be, that Christians and ministers of the Gospel shall arise *self-moved*, or rather moved by the spirit of Christ within them, and exert all their powers for the good of the perishing? when they shall not need appeal upon appeal, entreaty upon entreaty, and the visit of one agent after another, to remind them of duty, and to persuade them to do it?

It was not a world of penitents that the Saviour pitied, but a world of *rebels*—proud and stubborn rebels, ready to spurn every offer of reconciliation. He saw us, not on our knees pleading for mercy, but scorning the humble attitude of suppliants, and raising our puny arms against the authority of Heaven. He beheld us, not as the Ninevites once were, in sackcloth and ashes, but recklessly violating all his holy laws. It was in view of all the deformity, bitterness, rage and heaven-daring impiety of our naked hearts, that Christ left his throne of glory and died on the cross. It was for such beings that he voluntarily endured humiliation, toil, self-denial and death. He toiled and died for the ungodly. He came, though men despised his aid. He died even for his crucifiers. [Pg 27]

Are the heathen guilty—covered with blood and black with crime? Do they exhibit many traits that are repulsive and horrid? Would our visit to them fill them with rage and bitterness, and tempt them to crucify us? What then? are we to relax our efforts for them, because they are ungodly? So did *not* Jesus Christ. Let us learn from his example, and imbibe his spirit. That man, who may be called a missionary, and yet is capable of being alienated in his feelings by ill-treatment, contempt, abuse and rage from the heathen, is not worthy of the name. That professed Christian, in whatever land he may reside, who loves a sinner less on account of the personal abuse he may suffer from him, has not the true missionary spirit, or, in other words, the spirit of Christ.

And here I would repeat the remark with emphasis, in accordance with all that I have said, that *there is nothing peculiar* in the spirit of missions, except what peculiarity there may be in the spirit of Christ — that it is what all must possess to be disciples, and without which no one can enter heaven. It is a spirit humble yet elevating, self-sacrificing yet joyful, intensely fervent yet reasonable, meek [Pg 28] and yet resolute. It is all this indeed, but yet nothing more than what is required of every Christian; and therefore no excuse can be more absurd and contradictory in terms, than that sometimes made, "It is not my duty to go to the heathen, for I never had a missionary spirit;" for one professes to be a Christian, and yet excuses himself, on the ground of not having a missionary spirit, or in other words, of not being a Christian — of not being in possession of a fair title to heaven. O, remember, Christian reader, that the least desire to be excused shows a deplorable lack of the spirit of Christ.

CHAPTER II.

CHRISTIAN STEWARDSHIP.

On account of heavy domestic afflictions, and the failure of my own health, I was induced, a few years since, to visit the United States. Full well I remember my feelings when returning to my native land. I had been laboring among a heathen people, and [Pg 29] impressions by the eye are deep and affecting. I had seen degradation and vileness, destitution and woe. I had a vivid impression of the urgent claim of the destitute and the dying; and I had formed some conception of the greatness of the work, if we would put forth the instrumentality needed to elevate and save them. And during a long voyage, I had time, not only to think of the Sandwich Islanders, but to cast my thoughts abroad over the wide world. The millions and hundreds of millions of our race often came up fresh before me, sunk in untold vileness, covered with abominations, and dropping one after another, as fast as the beating of my pulse—twenty millions a year—into the world of woe. Painful as it was, I could not avoid the deep and certain conviction, that such was their end.

Then I thought of the greatness of the task, if we would be the means, under God, of saving them from perdition: that we have idol gods without number to destroy—a veil of superstition forty centuries thick to rend—a horrible darkness to dispel—hearts of stone to break—a gulf of pollution to purify—nations, in God's strength, to reform and regenerate. [Pg 30] With such thoughts the conviction forced itself upon me, that the work could not be done without an immense amount of means, and a host of laborers.

Think, then, how chilling and soul-sickening the intelligence that met me as I landed on my native shores, (in the spring of 1838,) that Christians were disheartened by the pressure of the times, and were receding from ground already taken: that the bread of life must not issue from the press, though millions were famishing for lack of it; that thirty heralds of salvation then standing on our shores must not embark, though the woes and agonies of dying souls were coming peal after peal on every wave of the ocean; that they must be turned aside from the perilous yet fond enterprise to which the love of Christ had constrained them, and that future applicants must be thereby discouraged—that missionaries abroad must be trammelled in their operations for want of means; and that multitudes of children and youth, the hope of the missions, gathered with much care, and partially instructed and trained with much expense of time, strength and money; the centre of solicitude, love, and interest; the [Pg 31] adopted sons and daughters of the missionaries, must be sent back—in Ceylon three thousand in a day—to wallow again in pollution, bow down to gods of wood and stone, and wander, stumble and fall on the dark mountains of heathen superstition; a prey to the prowling monsters that lie thick and ready to devour in all the territory of Satan. Surely, thought I, (and had I not grounds for the thought?) Christians in America must be destitute of the common comforts of life: nothing but the direst necessity can induce them thus to surrender back to Satan the ground already taken and the trophies already gathered, and to put far off the hope of the latter day glory.

I looked abroad and made inquiries. I found indeed a derangement of currency and a stagnation of business. But did I find, think you, that Christians were destitute of the ordinary comforts of life? that they were in a distressing emergency for food and clothing? that their retrenchments had been made *first* in personal expenditures, and last in efforts to save souls? Alas! it was evident that the principal cause of the retraced movement was not found in the reverse of the [Pg 32] times. It was found to lie deeper; and to consist in wrong views and wrong practice on the great subject of Christian stewardship. To this subject, then, my thoughts for a time were much directed, and I tried to look at it in view of a dying world, and a coming judgment. The subject, I perceived, lay at the foundation of all missionary effort; and my position and circumstances were perhaps advantageous for contemplating it in a just and proper light. Be entreated, therefore, Christian reader, to look at the subject in the spirit of candor and self-application.

A little heathen child was inquired of by her teacher, if there was anything which she could call her own. She hesitated a moment, and looking up, very humbly replied, "I think there is." "What is it?" asked the teacher. "I think," said she, "that my sins are my own."

Yes, we may claim our sins—they are our own; but everything else belongs to God. We are stewards; and a steward is one who is employed to manage the concerns of another—his household, money or estate. We are God's stewards. God has intrusted to [Pg 33] each one of us a charge of greater or less importance. To some he has intrusted five talents, to others two, and to others one. The talents are physical strength, property, intellect, learning, influence— all the means in our possession for doing good and glorifying God. We can lay claim to nothing as strictly our own. Even the angel Gabriel cannot claim the smallest particle of dust as strictly his own. The rightful owner of all things, great and small, is God.

To be faithful stewards, then, we must *fully occupy* for God all the talents in our possession. A surrender, however, of all to God — of time, strength, mind and property, does not imply a neglect of our own real wants. A proper care of ourselves and families enters into God's arrangement. This is not only allowed, it is required of us; and if done properly and with a right spirit, it is a service acceptable to God. This is understood then, when we say, that all our talents must be occupied for God. With this understanding, there must be no reserve. Reserve is robbery. No less than all the heart and all our powers can be required of us — no less can be required of angels.

It is our reasonable service. We require the same of the agents we [Pg 34] employ. Suppose a steward, agent or clerk, in the management of your money, your estate or your goods, devotes only a part to your benefit and uses the rest for himself, how long would you retain him in your employment? Let us beware, then, that we rob not God. Let us be faithful in his business, and *fully occupy* for him the talents intrusted to us. God has an indisputable right to everything in our possession; to all our strength, all our influence, every moment of our time, and demands that everything be held loosely by us, in perfect obedience to him. For us or for angels to deny this right, would be downright rebellion. For God to require anything less, would be admitting a principle that would demolish his throne.

No less engagedness certainly can be required of God's stewards, than *worldly men exhibit in the pursuit of wealth and honor.* Let us, then, look at their conduct and learn a lesson. They are intent upon their object. They rise early and sit up late. Constant toil and vigorous exertion fill up the day, and on their beds at night they meditate plans for the [Pg 35] morrow. Their hearts are set on their object, and entirely engrossed in it. They show a determination to attain it, if it be within the compass of human means. Enter a Merchants' Exchange, and see with what fixed application they study the best plans of conducting their business. They keep their eyes and ears open, and their thoughts active. Such, too, must be the wakefulness of an agent, or they will not employ him. Notice also the physician who aspires to eminence. He tries the utmost of his skill. Look in, too, upon the ambitious attorney. He applies his mind closely to his cause that he may manage it in the best possible way.

Now, I ask, shall not the same intense and active state of mind be required of us, as God's agents or stewards? Can we be faithful stewards, and not contrive, study, and devise the best ways of using the talents that God has intrusted to us, so that they may turn to the greatest account in his service? Is not the glory of God and the eternal salvation of our ruined race, an object *worthy* of as much engagedness, as much engrossment of soul and determination of purpose, as a little property which must soon be wrapped in flames, or the [Pg 36] flickering breath of empty fame? Be assured, we cannot satisfy our Maker by offering a sluggish service, or by putting forth a little effort, and pretending that it is the extent of our ability. We have shown what we are capable of doing, by our engagedness in seeking wealth and honor. God has seen, angels have seen, and we ourselves know, that our ability is not small, when brought fully into exercise. It is now too late to indulge the thought of deceiving either our Maker or our fellow men on this point. We can lay claim to the character of faithful stewards, only as we *embark all our powers* in serving God, as worldly men do in seeking riches, or a name.

Then, too, to be faithful, we must be as *enterprising* in the work that God has given us to do, as worldly men are in their affairs. By enterprising, I mean, bold, adventurous, resolute to undertake. Worldly men exhibit enterprise in their readiness to engage in large projects—in digging canals, in laying railroads, and in sending their ships around the globe. No port seems too distant, no depth too deep, no height too high, no difficulty too great, and no obstacle too formidable. They scarcely shrink from any business on account [Pg 37] of its magnitude, its arduousness, or its hazard. A man is no longer famous for circumnavigating the globe. To sail round the world is a common trading voyage, and ships now visit almost every port of the whole earth. A business is no longer called great, where merely thousands of dollars are adventured; but in great undertakings, money is counted by millions. Such is the spirit of enterprise in worldly matters.

Now, I ask, are we not capable of as much enterprise in using the means ordained by Christ for rescuing souls from eternal burnings, and raising them to a seat at his right hand? Had the same enterprise been required of men in some former century, they might have plead incapacity. But it is too late now to plead incapacity.

Unless we choose to keep back from God a very important talent, we must put forth this enterprise to its full extent in the great work of the world's conversion.

Such enterprise is needed. If the latter day glory is to take place through human instrumentality, can it be expected without some mighty movement on the part of the church? Can a work of such inconceivable magnitude [Pg 38] be effected, till every redeemed sinner shall lay himself out in the enterprise, as worldly men do in their projects? If the promises of God are to be fulfilled through the efforts of men, what hope can there be of the glorious day, till men are resolute to undertake great things—not for themselves merely, but for God, their Maker and Redeemer.

Is it not a fact that will strike us dumb in the judgment, that it is the love of money, and not zeal for God, that digs canals, lays railroads, runs steamboats and packets, and, in short, is the main spring of every great undertaking? The love of money has explored the land and the seas, traced rivers in all their windings, found an entrance to almost every port, Christian or heathen, studied the character of almost every people, ascertained the products of every clime and the treasures of the deep, stationed agents in all the principal places, and in not a few ports, a hemisphere distant, erected shops, factories, and even sumptuous palaces.

Men exhibit no such enterprise in serving God. How many ships sail the ocean to carry the Gospel of Christ? And in ports where one magnificent Exchange after an [Pg 39] other is reared, stretching out its capacious arms, and towering towards heaven, how difficult it is to sustain a few humble boarding-houses for wandering seamen. Worldly enterprise is bold and active, and presses onward with railroad speed. Shall, then, Christian enterprise be dull and sluggish, deal in cents and mills, and move along at a very slow pace? The thought is too humiliating to be endured.

Suppose angels to be placed in our stead, would they, think you, be outdone by the seekers of wealth in deeds of enterprise? No: their cars would be the first in motion, and their ships the first on the wing. They would be the first to announce new islands, and the first to project improvements, and *for what?* that the Gospel might have free course and be glorified. Enterprise and action would then be exhibited, worthy of our gaze and admiration. "O! if the ransom of those who fell from heaven like stars to eternal night, could only be paid, and the inquiry of the Lord were heard among the unfallen, 'Whom shall we send, and who will go for us?' hold they back? No: they fly like lightning to every province of hell; the echo of salvation [Pg 40] rolls in the outskirts as in the centre; a light shines in the darkest dungeon; the heaviest chains are knocked off, and they rest not till all is done that angels can do, to restore them to their former vacated seats in the realms of the blest."

But if angels would act thus, we too, as the stewards of God, ought to be the first in enterprise. God's work is infinitely more important than wealth or honor. And how shall we, in the judgment, be found faithful, if the seekers of wealth or the aspirants for renown are suffered to outstrip us on every side.

It is not faithfulness for any one to consume *on himself or his children* more of God's property than he really needs. Suppose you hold in your hand an amount of property. It is not yours you remember, for you are merely a steward. God requires that it be used to produce the greatest possible good. The greatest possible good, is the promotion of holiness in yourself and in others. Luxury, pride and vanity can lay no claim. Speculative knowledge, taste, and refinement must receive a due share of attention, but be kept in their place. Our real wants, of course, must be supplied. But what are our real [Pg 41] wants—our *wants*, not our *desires*—our *real* wants, not those that are artificial and imaginary?

We really need for ourselves and families what is necessary to preserve life and health; we need a mental cultivation answerable to our profession or employment; need the means of maintaining a neat, sober and just taste; and we need too, proper advantages of spiritual improvement. Things of mere habit, fashion, and fancy may be dispensed with. Luxuries may be denied. Many things, which are called conveniences, we do not really need. If provision is to be made for all things that are convenient and pleasant, what room will remain for self-denial? Things deemed comfortable and convenient may be multiplied without limit—consume all of God's wealth, and leave the world in ruins. If the world were *not* in ruins, then it might be proper to seek not only the comforts, but even the elegancies of life.

Take a simple illustration: In the midst of the wide ocean I fall in with a crew floating on the few shattered planks of a hopeless wreck. I have a supply of water and a cask of bread, but the poor wrecked mariners are [Pg 42] entirely destitute. Shall I keep my provisions for my own comfort, and leave these sufferers to pine away with hunger and thirst? But suppose I have not only bread and water, but many luxuries, while the men on the wreck are perishing for the want of a morsel of bread and a drop of water? And then, suppose I have casks of bread and other provisions to dispose of, and intend with the proceeds to furnish myself with certain of the conveniences and elegancies of life; and my mind is so fixed upon obtaining them, that I refuse to relieve the poor tenants of the wreck, and leave them to the lingering death of hunger and thirst. O, who of you would not shudder at the hardness of my heart and the blackness of my crime!

But the world dead in sin is surely a wreck. Millions upon millions are famishing for the bread and water of life. Their cry — their dying cry has come to our ears. Shall we then take that which might relieve them, and expend it in procuring conveniences, elegancies, and luxuries for ourselves? Can we do it, and be guiltless of blood?

But, perhaps here, some one may have the coolness to thrust in the common objection, [Pg 43] that a man's style of living must correspond with his station in society. It is wonderful to what an extent this principle is applied. A man, it is said, cannot be a governor of a state, a mayor of a city, a member of Congress, or hold any high office, unless his house, his equipage, his dress and his table, exhibit some appearance of elegance and wealth; and if a man live in a large and opulent city, he must be somewhat expensive in his style of living, that he may exert an influence in the higher walks of society. Then, country towns, and small villages, take pattern of the large cities, and the plea goes down through every rank and every grade. Scarcely a Christian can be found, who is not familiar with the doctrine. It is a very convenient doctrine. In a *qualified* sense it may be true, but in its unlimited interpretation it may be made to justify almost every article of luxury and extravagance.

It seems to be conformity to the world, and the world has always been *wrong*. The principles of the Gospel have always been at variance with the maxims and customs of the world. *Conformity is always suspicious.*

Again, the doctrine cannot be applied to all places. Suppose a missionary conform to the [Pg 44] society around him. Instead of raising up the heathen from their degradation, he would become a heathen himself. The descent to heathenism is easy. The influence of comparing ourselves with ourselves, and measuring ourselves by ourselves, is felt by those living among barbarians as well as at home, though the insidious influence leads in another direction. If there is a man on earth, who, more than any other, needs to cultivate neatness, taste and refinement, both in his mind and in his whole style of living, it is the man who is surrounded by a heathen population. Here, then, the rule contended for fails. Travel round the world, and how often will it fail?

Let us turn away, then, from this fickle standard, and look to reason enlightened by the Word of God. Shall we not then find, that substantially the same style of living that is proper in one latitude and longitude, is proper in another; *substantially* the same, paying only so much regard to the eyes of the world, as to avoid unnecessary singularity and remark; and that this rule, founded on the principles of the Gospel, makes a proper provision for health, mental cultivation, and a [Pg 45] neat, sober and just taste? Are not these the real wants of men allowed by the Gospel, whether they live in London or in Ethiopia?

But the ground on which I choose to rest this inquiry more than any other, is the perishing condition of our dying race. Is fashion, splendor and parade, appropriate in a grave-yard, or in the chamber of the dead and dying? But the whole world is a grave-yard. Countless millions lie beneath our feet. Most of our earth, too, is at this moment a chamber of dying souls. Can we have *any relish* for luxuries, folly and needless expense, amidst the teeming millions commencing the agonies of eternal death?

I erect a splendid mansion; extend about it a beautiful enclosure; furnish it with every elegance; make sumptuous entertainments, and live in luxury and ease. In the midst of it, the woes and miseries of my ruined race are brought vividly before me—their present wretchedness and eternal agonies. And it is whispered in my ear, that these woes might have been relieved by the expense I have so profusely lavished. O! how like Belshazzar must I feel, and almost imagine that the groans of lost souls are echoed in every chamber of [Pg 46] my mansion, and their blood seen on every ornament!

Let us have the love of Christ in our hearts, and then spread distinctly before us *the world as it is*—calculate the sum total of its present wretchedness and eternal woes. In such a world and as God's stewards, who can be at a loss in regard to the course of duty? When twenty millions of men every year are entering upon the untold horrors of the second death, and we are stewards to employ all means in our power for their salvation, O, away with that coldness that can suggest the necessity of *conforming* to the expensive customs of the world. May we, in heaven, find one of these souls saved through our instrumentality, and we can afford to forego all we shall lose by a want of conformity. There is a nobleness in taking an independent stand on the side of economy, and saving something to benefit dying souls. There is a heavenly dignity in such a course, infinitely superior to the slavish conformity so much contended for. It is an independence induced by the sublimest motives; a stand which even the world must respect, and which God will not fail to honor.

But how shall those possessing *large capi* [Pg 47] *tals* best employ them as stewards of God? I speak not of the hoarding of the miser; that would be a waste of breath. I speak not of property invested in stock that habitually violates the Sabbath. No remark is necessary in so plain a case. But I speak of large capitals, professedly kept to bring in an income for the service of the Redeemer. The subject is involved in many practical difficulties; and they who are business men have some advantages of judging in the case which I have not. I will therefore merely make one or two inquiries.

Is not the practice in many cases an *unwise investment* of God's funds? Is there not a reasonable prospect that one dollar used now, in doing good, will turn to more account than twenty dollars ten years hence? A Bible given now may be the means of a soul's conversion; and this convert may be instrumental in converting other souls, and may consecrate all his powers and property to God; so that when years shall have passed away, the one dollar given to buy the Bible may have become hundreds of dollars, and, with God's blessing, saved many precious souls. One pious young man trained for the ministry *now*, [Pg 48] may be instrumental, before ten years shall expire, in bringing into the Lord's kingdom many immortal souls, with all their wealth and influence; and so the small sum expended now, become ten years hence entirely inestimable. The same may be said of a minister sent now to the heathen, instead of ten years hence; and the same, too, may be said of every department of doing good. It would appear then, that, in all ordinary cases, to make an immediate use of funds in doing good is to lay them out to the greatest possible interest; that by such a course we can be the means of peopling heaven faster than in any other way. We can hardly appreciate how much we save by saving *time*, and how much we lose by losing it. Worldly men, in their railroad and steam-packet spirit of the present day, seem to have caught some just sense of the importance of time, and we, in our enterprises to do good, must not be unmindful of it.

Again, is not the expenditure of property in the work of doing good, not only the most advantageous, but also the *safest* possible investment of God's funds? Whilst kept in capital, it is always exposed to greater or less risk. Fire may consume it. Floods may [Pg 49] sweep it away. Dishonest men may purloin it. A gale at sea may bury it. A reverse of times may ingulf it. But when used in doing good, it is sent up to the safe-keeping of the bank of God; it is commuted into the precious currency of heaven; it is exchanged for souls made happy, and harps and crowns of gold.

Again, A. keeps a large property in capital, and therefore B. resolves to *accumulate* a large property, and then give the income. But whilst accumulating it, he not only leaves the world to perish, but also runs the risk of ruining his own soul—the awful hazard which always attends the project of becoming rich. And the result is, in ninety-nine cases out of a hundred, that the summons of death arrives before the promised beneficence is paid in.

In view of such considerations, would it not be *wiser, safer, and very much better*, in most instances at least, that the greater part of large capitals should be made use of at once in the service of the Redeemer?

It is said of Normand Smith, that "he dared not be rich;" and that "it became an established rule with him, to use for benevolent distribution *all the means* which he could take [Pg 50] from his business, and still prosecute it successfully;" and that he charged a brother on his dying bed, to do good with his substance while living, and not suffer it to accumulate to be disposed of, at the last extremity, by will. Sound advice. A few other such men there have been in the world, and they are the shining lights. Their example is brilliant all over with true wisdom.

It is not acting always as faithful stewards, merely to accumulate wealth to promote the cause of Christ; for there may be more need of our *personal service* in disseminating the Gospel, than of any pecuniary means we can contribute. Christians are not faithful stewards, merely when they labor for Christ, but when they do *that* by which they may most promote the cause of Christ. The dissemination of Gospel truth is the great end to be aimed at, either directly or indirectly. Now, it is evident that many must further this object by accumulating the pecuniary means; but the danger is, that too many, far too many prefer this course. Many conclude, with perfect safety and justness, that in practising law or medicine, or in selling goods, in tilling a farm, or in laboring in a shop, they are doing [Pg 51] as much to further the object as in any other way; but some, it is believed, come to such a conclusion either from mistaken views or mistaken motives. The fact that so large a proportion of God's stewards resort to the notion of operating by proxy, and that so few choose to engage in the direct work, shows that there is danger existing. Not only the fathers, but a vast majority of the middle aged and the young, prefer to advance the cause of Christ by accumulating the pecuniary means. Now, why is there such a rushing after this department of the great work?

The Saviour calls for a great army of preachers, to carry his Gospel everywhere, and to proclaim it to all nations, kindreds and people. In truth, you need not go beyond the limits of the United States to feel the force of this remark. Look at the destitutions in the more newly settled states and territories, and see if there is not need of men to preach the Gospel. But notwithstanding this need, only a small number, comparatively, offer themselves to the work. Almost all young men, even the professedly pious, slide easily into lucrative occupations; but to bring them into the direct work of making known Christ, [Pg 52] they must be urged and persuaded by a score of arguments.

It is needed, too, of lay members of the church, to do much in searching out the destitute and the dying, who exist in multitudes, even about their own dwellings; to give here a word of warning, and there a word of consolation; to add here a helping hand, and impart there the restoring effect of sympathy and kindness; in short, to employ some hours in the day in going everywhere, as the early disciples did, from house to house and street to street, and in communicating, in an appropriate way, the simple truths of Jesus. Laymen, too, are needed in great numbers in the foreign service. There are reasons numerous and urgent, which I cannot here name, why lay members in the church should go abroad.

But notwithstanding this call for personal effort, it is too often that we meet with church members who are completely engrossed, from early dawn to the close of day, in accumulating wealth; and who deny themselves the luxury of spending either hour of the twenty-four, in conversing with souls, and leading them to Jesus. Such persons will give somewhat of their substance, when called upon; [Pg 53] and press on, almost out of breath apparently, in the cares of the world, not thinking to say to this man or that, on the right hand and the left, that there is a heaven above and a hell beneath, and death is at the door. You would almost imagine, from the conduct of some, that they would like to commit to proxy even their own faith and repentance. Now this entire engrossment in worldly cares, even though professedly for Christ's sake, will never illumine the dark recesses of the earth—will never usher in the millenial day.

It is not so much, after all, an accumulation of wealth that is needed, as the personal engagement of Christians in making known everywhere, at home and abroad, the precious news of Jesus. The disposition to go everywhere, regardless of wealth, and with Jesus on our lips, must be the spirit of the church, before we can expect much good either at home or abroad. The world will not be covered with the knowledge of the Lord as the waters cover the sea, till men to make known that word are scattered like rain on all the earth—not only in heathen lands, but in the streets and lanes of large cities, and throughout the Western desolations. "So [Pg 54] long as we remain together, like water in a lake, so long the moral world will be desolate. We must go everywhere, and if the expansive warmth of benevolence will not separate us, so that we arise and go on the wings of the wind, God, be assured, will break up the fountains of the great deep of society, and dashing the parts together, like ocean in his turmoil or Niagara in its fall, cover the heavens with showers, and set the bow of hope for the nations, and the desert shall rejoice and blossom as the rose. God is too good to suffer either Amazon or Superior to lie still, and become corrupt, and the heavens in consequence to be brass and the earth iron." God is too benevolent also, in the arrangements of the moral world, to allow his people to be inactive—to have here a continuing city, and be immersed in the cares of the world as though here were their treasure, while thousands about them are dying for lack of instruction, and the heathen abroad are going down to death in one unbroken phalanx. The church must take more exercise, and the proper kind, too, or she will become frail and sickly, too weak in prayer, and too ignorant in effort to usher in the millenial day. [Pg 55]

It is a possible thing to seek wealth *honestly* for God; but he that is called to such a work, has more occasion to mourn than to rejoice: he has occasion to tremble, watch, and pray; for to be a faithful steward of God's property, requires perhaps more grace than to be a faithful steward of God's truth. We find many a faithful preacher of the Gospel where we find one Normand Smith, or Nathaniel R. Cobb, or one firm of Homes & Homer. The grace needed is so great, and the temptations to err so many, that almost all prove defaulters, and therefore it is that the world lies in ruins: not because the church has not wealth enough, but because God's stewards claim to be owners.

How small the sum appropriated by a million and a half of God's stewards to save a sinking world! The price of earthly ambition, convenience and pleasure, is counted by millions. Navies and armies have their millions; railroads and canals have their millions; colleges and schools have their millions; silks, carpets and mirrors, have their millions; parties of pleasure and licentiousness in high life and in low life have their millions; and what has the treasury of God and the Lamb, to [Pg 56] redeem a world of souls from the pains of eternal damnation, and to fill them with joys unspeakable? The sum is so small in comparison that one's tongue refuses to utter it.

There must be a different scale of giving; and the only way to effect it is, to induce a different style of personal consecration. Let a man give himself, or rather let him have a heart that cannot *refrain* from telling of Jesus to those who are near, or from going to those who are more remote, and the mere item of property you will find appended, as a matter of course, and on the plain principle that the greater always includes the less. We must learn to devote, according to our vows, time, talents, body, soul and spirit. Bodies and minds are wanted; the bones and sinews of men are required: these more substantial things are needed, as well as property, in arduous services at home and still more self-denying labor abroad; and no redeemed sinner can refuse either the one or the other, and continue to be regarded as a faithful steward of Jesus. *Money, though needed, is by no means all that is required of us.*

Though God has devolved upon us, as stewards, a responsible work, the weight of [Pg 57] which is fearful, and sufficient to crush us unless aided from on high, yet the employment is one of *indescribable delight*. It is a pleasant work. Angels would rejoice to be so employed.

Is there any professed Christian who does not relish the idea? To such an one I would say, Your condition is by no means enviable. You deny yourself all true happiness. If you do not delight in the thought of being God's steward; of holding not only property, but body, soul and spirit at God's control, then you know not what true luxury is. There is pleasure in doing good; there is a luxury in entire consecration to God. The pleasures of this earth are empty, vain and fleeting; but the pleasure of doing good is real, substantial and enduring. The pleasure of doing good is the joy of angels; it is the thrill of delight which pervades the soul of Jesus; it is the happiness of the eternal God. In not wishing to be God's steward, you deny yourself this luxury; you refuse angels' food and feed on husks. O, there is a richness of holy joy in yielding up all to God, and holding ourselves as waiting servants to do his will. This fullness of bliss you foolishly spurn from you, and [Pg 58] turn away to the "beggarly elements of the world." Do you feel that the principles of stewardship contained in the Bible are too strict — that too entire a devotement is required of you? Angels do not think so. Redeemed saints do not think so. The more entire the consecration, the more perfect the bliss. In heaven devotement is perfect, and joy of course unalloyed. Blot out this spirit of consecration, you blot out all true happiness on earth; you annihilate heaven.

But it is not only a luxury, but *an honor* to be the stewards of God. What honor greater than that of continuing the work which Jesus commenced; of being employed in the immense business of saving a ruined race? What work more glorious than that of being the instruments of peopling heaven? What employment more noble than to rescue immortal souls from endless agonies, and to raise them to eternal joys; to take their feet from the sides of the burning lake, and to plant them on the firm pavement of heaven; to rescue victims from eternal burnings, and to place them as gems in the diadem of God? Would not Gabriel feel himself honored with a work so noble and glorious? Were a presidency or [Pg 59] a kingdom offered you, spurn it and be wise; but contemn not the glory of being God's stewards.

Remember, too, whether these are your views or not, the work of God will go on. The world will be converted. The glorious event is promised. Almighty power and infinite wisdom are engaged to accomplish it: all the resources of heaven are pledged. The God of heaven, he will prosper his true servants, and they shall arise and build; but those who do not relish the idea of being God's stewards, can have no portion, nor right, nor memorial in Jerusalem. The wheels of God's providence are rolling onward: those wheels are high and dreadful. Will you, being a professed Christian, dare to oppose the march of God? "Ah! we do not *oppose*," say you. But I reply, There can be no neutrality; you must either help onward his car of victory, or you do really stand in the way — will be crushed by his power, and ground into the earth by the weight of his chariot. Take then, I entreat you, this warning, which is given you in earnestness, but in the spirit of love.

Joy, glory and immortality, to all who will [Pg 60] cordially assent to be co-workers with Jesus. They shall ride with him in his chariot from conquering to conquer, and shall sit with him on his throne in the day of triumph.

Be entreated, then, professed Christian, first to give your own soul to the Lord, and with your soul all you have, all you are, and all you hope to be. Make an entire consecration. You will never regret having done so, in time or in eternity.

May God give us all grace to imbibe wholly the true principles of stewardship. Not the principles popular in the world, but the principles of the Bible; those principles which hold out the only hope of the latter day glory — of means commensurate with so great an end.

CHAPTER III.

GUILT OF NEGLECTING THE HEATHEN.

During all the years that I have been allowed to labor for the heathen, my mind has been led to contemplate, constantly and intensely, the obligations of Christian nations [Pg 61] towards those who sit in darkness; obligations arising from the command of Christ, and the principles of the Gospel. And I shall, therefore, in this chapter, freely, fully, and solemnly express the sentiments which have been maturing in my mind, on the *great guilt* which Christians incur in *neglecting the heathen.*

The heathen world, as a mass, has been left to perish. And by whom? Not by the Father of mercies; he gave his Son to redeem it: not by the Saviour of sinners; look at Calvary: not by the Holy Spirit; his influences have been ever ready: not by angels; their wings have never tired when sent on errands of mercy. All that Heaven could do has been done, consistently with the all-wise arrangement of committing an important agency to the church. The church has been slothful and negligent. Each generation of Christians has in turn received the vast responsibility, neglected it in a great measure, and transmitted it to the next. The *guilt* of this neglect who can estimate?

That such neglect is highly criminal, the Bible everywhere testifies. It says, "If thou forbear to deliver them that are drawn unto [Pg 62] death, and those that are ready to be slain; if thou sayest, Behold, we knew it not; doth not he that pondereth the heart consider it? and he that keepeth thy soul, doth not he know it?" And shall not he "render to every man according to his works?" This solemn interrogation needs no comment. The obvious import is, *If our fellow men are perishing, and we neglect to do what we can to save them, we are guilty of their blood.* But this testimony does not stand alone. What does God say to the prophet, who should see the peril of the wicked, and neglect to save him by giving him warning? "His blood will I require at thy hand." What does God say of the watchman of a city who should see the sword come, and blow not the trumpet? "If the sword come and take any person from among them, his blood will I require at the watchman's hand."

But this is not only the sentiment of the Bible, but the voice of common sense.

A neighbor of mine is drowning in the river. With a little exertion I can save his life, but neglect to do it. Shall I escape the goadings of conscience and the charge of blood-guiltiness? [Pg 63]

A house is in flames. The perishing occupants, looking from a window, implore of me to reach them a ladder. I have some little affairs of my own to attend to, and turn a deaf ear to their cry. The flames gather around them: they throw themselves from the window, and are dashed in pieces on the pavement. Who will not charge me with the loss of those lives?

To-day, a raging malady is spreading through the streets of a large city. The people are dying by hundreds. I know the cause; the fountains of the city are poisoned. From indolence, or some other cause, I neglect to give the information, and merely attend to my own safety. Who would not load me with the deepest guilt, and stamp me as the basest of murderers?

Both Scripture and common sense, then, concur in establishing the sentiment, that if our fellow men are perishing, and we neglect to do what we can to save them, we are guilty of their blood. But if this doctrine be true, its application to Christians, in the relation which they sustain to the heathen world, is irresistibly conclusive and awfully momentous. The soul shudders, and shrinks back from the [Pg 64] fearful thought: If six hundred millions of our race are sinking to perdition, and we neglect to do what we can to save them, we shall be found accountable for their eternal agonies.

If such a charge is standing against us, we shall soon meet it. The day of judgment will soon burst upon us. Let us look, then, at the subject candidly, prayerfully, and with a desire to do our duty.

The conditions on which the charge impends are simply two: that the heathen world are sinking to perdition, and that we are neglecting to do what we can to save them. If these two points are substantiated, the overwhelming conclusion is inevitable. It becomes us, then, to look well at these points—to examine them with faithfulness and with honesty.

Is it true, that *the heathen world are sinking to perdition*? As fast as the beating of my pulse, they are passing into the world of retribution, and the inquiry is, What is the doom they meet? Do they rise to unite with angels in the songs of heaven? or sink in ceaseless and untold misery?

Certain it is, that they are not saved through [Pg 65] faith in Christ; for "how shall they believe in him of whom they have not heard?" It is also clear that God, in his usual method, does not bestow the gift of repentance and eternal life where a Saviour is not known. "It pleases God by the foolishness of preaching to save them that believe." Those who are saved, are said to be "begotten by the word of truth"—"born of the word of God." As the heathen nations, therefore, are not furnished with the appointed means of salvation, it follows inevitably that, as a mass at least, they are sinking to perdition. They are the "nations which have forgotten God," and "shall be turned into hell."

It is unnecessary to enter into the inquiry, whether it is possible, in the nature of the case, for a heathen unacquainted with the Gospel to be saved. It is sufficient to know the fact, that God has ordained the preaching of the Gospel as the means of saving the nations; and that there is probably no instance on record, which may not be called in question, of a heathen being converted without a knowledge of the true God and of his Son Jesus Christ.

But the consideration, solemn and conclu [Pg 66] sive, which needs no other to corroborate it or render it overwhelming, is the *character* of the heathen. Look at their character, as portrayed by the Apostle Paul in the first chapter to the Romans. Read the whole chapter, but especially the conclusion, where he describes the heathen as "being filled with all unrighteousness, fornication, wickedness, covetousness, maliciousness; full of envy, murder, debate, deceit, malignity; whisperers, back-biters, haters of God, despiteful, proud, boasters, inventors of evil things, disobedient to parents, without understanding, covenant breakers, without natural affection, implacable, unmerciful." This description is not understood in Christian lands, neither can it be; but missionaries to the heathen, who are eye-witnesses of what is here described, place an emphasis on every epithet, and would clothe every word in capitals.

The character of the heathen is no better now than in the days of Paul. It is *worse*. It is impossible that such a state of society should remain stationary. A mortal disease becomes more and more malignant, till a remedy is applied; a sinking weight hastens downwards with continually accumulating [Pg 67] force; and mind, thrown from its balance, wanders farther and farther from reason. It is thus with the disease of sin, the downward propensities of a depraved nature, and a soul revolted from God. Besides, Satan has not been inactive in heathen lands. He has been aware that efforts would be made to save them. And night and day, year after year, and age after age, he has sought, with ceaseless toil and consummate skill, to perfect the heathen in every species of iniquity, harden their hearts to every deed of cruelty, sink them to the lowest depths of pollution and degradation, and place them at the farthest remove from the possibility of salvation. It is impossible to describe the state of degradation and unblushing sin to which the nations, for ages sinking, have sunk, and to which Satan in his undisturbed exertions for centuries has succeeded in reducing them. It is impossible to give a representation of their unrestrained passions, the abominations connected with their idol worship, or the scenes of discord, cruelty and blood, which everywhere abound. I speak of those lands where the Gospel has not been extended. Truly darkness covers such lands, and gross darkness [Pg 68] the people. Deceit, oppression and cruelty fill every hut with woe; and impurity deluges the land like an overflowing stream. Neither can it be said, that the conduct of the heathen becomes sinless through ignorance. From observation for many years, I can assert that they have consciences—that they feel accountable for what they do.

Will, then, God transplant the vine of Sodom, unchanged in its nature, to overrun his paradise above? Will he open the gates of his holy city, and expose the streets of its peaceful inhabitants to those whose heart is cruelty, whose visage is scarred with fightings, and whose hands are red with blood? "Know ye not, that the unrighteous shall not enter into the kingdom of heaven?" Where, then, is the hope of the unconverted heathen? If there were *innocent* heathen, as some men are ready to imagine in the face of God's word, and in the face of a flood of facts, then indeed they might be saved without the Gospel. But this mass of pollution, under which the earth groans, must disgorge itself into the pit of woe. We cannot evade the conclusion, painful as it is, that the millions of this world of sin are sinking to perdition.

The American churches have peculiar advantages to carry abroad the [Pg 69] Gospel of Christ; and ability in such an enterprise is the measure of our duty. "If there be first a willing mind, it is accepted according to that a man hath, and not according to that he hath not." "To whom much is given of him will much be required." And to determine whether Christians in the United States are *doing what they can* to save the heathen from their awful doom, the second point of inquiry proposed, it is necessary to look at their unparalleled advantages.

It may be said then, that Christians in America are not trammeled in their efforts to do good by any governmental restrictions, or ecclesiastical establishment. The remark is trite, but no less true, that the genius of our free constitution is eminently propitious to call forth energy and enterprise. And the remark applies with no more force to worldly matters, than to the business of doing good. The religion of Christ courts no extraneous influence, and is dependent for its power on no earthly aid. Under our free government, uncontrolled, unrestrained and unsupported, it is left to exert its own free and native energy. [Pg 70] We can plead, therefore, no arbitrary hindrance of any kind in the work of propagating the Gospel. And we can carry the Gospel, too, disconnected from any prejudicial alliance with political interests. This is the free, disencumbered, and unshackled condition in which the Gospel is permitted to have free course in our beloved land; and it is a talent put into our hands to be improved.

Again, no country possesses such advantages of education as the United States. In no land is knowledge so generally diffused throughout the different grades of society, and in no land do such facilities exist for acquiring a thorough education. Schools, colleges and seminaries, are open equally to the high and to the low, to the rich and to the poor; and only a good share of energy is required, to rise from any grade or condition of society, to eminence in general learning or professional study. The general intelligence of the community is such, that nothing but *disinclination* can prevent men from being acquainted with the wants of the world, and their duty to evangelize it; and the facilities for fitting themselves for the work are such, that nothing but criminal delinquency can hold back a very [Pg 71] large army from entering the field. This is an immense advantage committed to the American churches, for propagating the religion of Christ. It is another very precious talent committed to their trust, which if they fail to improve, they treasure up guilt.

Again, the American churches possess a great advantage in the facilities so generally enjoyed for accumulating wealth. The road to comfort and to affluence is open to all; and notwithstanding all reverses, the remark, as a general one, is still true, that the prosperity of the United States — of the whole mass of the people — is altogether unexampled, and that enterprise is vigorous and successful. In the greatest strait, how much retrenchment has there been in the style of living? And as we look into the future we see, (God's providence favoring,) that wealth is destined to flow in upon the land like a broad and deep river. Look at the extent of territory, bounded only by two rolling oceans; and at the resources which from year to year are developed — varied, unnumbered, and inexhaustible. If then unto whom much is given, of them will much be required, what may not God justly demand of American Christians? [Pg 72]

Another advantage which the American church possesses, is the Spirit which has been poured out upon her from on high. God has been pleased to bless her with precious revivals. The Holy Ghost has come down frequently and with power, and gathered in multitudes of souls. What God has wrought for the American Zion has been told in all lands, and every one applies the Saviour's injunction, "Freely ye have received—freely give." One great reason, perhaps, why the blessings of the Spirit are not now more richly enjoyed, is the neglect of Christians to make this return, and to labor gratefully for the destitute and the dying. It *was expected*, and justly too, that the land of apostolic revivals would be the first to imitate the apostles in the work of saving the heathen. A failure to do this may bring a blight upon the churches, if it has not brought it upon them already.

Surely, if there is a nation on earth to whom are intrusted many talents, ours is that nation. Our ability is not small. We must come up to a high measure of Christian action, before it can be said with truth, that we are *doing what we can* to save our ruined race. The United States, a nation planted by God, [Pg 73] enriched by his providence, nourished by his Holy Spirit, and brought to the strength of manhood in this solemnly momentous time of the nineteenth century, seems to have committed to her in a special manner the work of the world's conversion. Who knoweth but that she is brought to her preëminent advantages for such a time as this—for the interesting period preceding the latter day glory; and now if she prove herself unworthy of so lofty and responsible a trust, and neglect to put forth her strength to usher in the glorious day, deliverance will break out from some other quarter, but she, like a third Babylon, may sink in the bottomless abyss. An immense responsibility rests upon us. O that God would give us grace to act worthy of our trust—*to do what we can* for a dying world!

Let us inquire, then, Do we *pray* for the heathen as much as we ought? Were one duly impressed with the condition of perishing millions, certainly no less could be expected of him, than to fall on his knees many times a day, and to lift up his cry of earnest entreaty on their behalf. Filled with the love of Christ, and having distinctly and constantly before his mind the image of millions of im [Pg 74] mortal souls dropping into perdition, surely he could not refrain from an agony of prayer. Under such a sense of the wants and woes of our perishing race, a sense true to facts, he would have no rest.

But what prayer has actually been offered to the Lord for benighted nations? Is it not a fact, that many professed Christians do not remember the heathen once a day, and some not even once a month? Let the closet, the family altar, and the monthly concert testify. Prayer-meetings for the heathen—how thinly attended! what spectacles of grief to Jesus, and to angels! And if that prayer only is honest which is proved to be so by a readiness to labor, give, and go, there is reason to fear that few prayers for the heathen have been such that Christ could accept them, place them in his golden censer, and present them before the throne.

Since such is the case, what wonder is it that a million and a half of Christians in the United States should be so inefficient? Inefficient, I say, for what do this million and a half of professed Christians accomplish? By their vows they are bound to be as self-denying, as spiritual and devoted, as though they [Pg 75] were missionaries to foreign lands. If we should send abroad a million and a half of missionaries, we should expect that, under God, they would soon be the instruments of converting all nations. But what, in fact, does this vast number of professed Christians—or in other words, of the *professedly missionary band* of Jesus Christ, accomplish in the narrow limits of the United States? O, there is a deplorable lack in the churches, of the deep devotion and missionary character of our ascended Saviour.

Again, Do we *give* as much as we ought to evangelize the heathen? It would perhaps be a liberal estimate to say, that a million and a half of professed Christians in the United States give, on an average, year by year, to save the heathen, about twenty-four cents each, or two cents a month. There are other objects, it is true, that call for contributions; but put all contributions together, and how small the amount?

The Jews were required to give to religious objects at least one-fifth of their income. One-fifth of the income of a million and a half of Christians at seven per cent., supposing them to be worth on an average five hundred dol [Pg 76] lars each, would be ten and a half millions of dollars. This is merely the income of capital of which we now speak. A fifth of the income from trade and industry would probably double the amount, and make it twenty-one millions. Is anything like this sum given by American Christians to support and propagate the religion of Jesus? What Christians have done, therefore, is by no means a measure of their ability.

To see what men can do, it is necessary to look away from Christians, to those whose ruling principle is a thirst for pleasure, for honor, and for gain. How vast a sum is expended at theatres—on fashionable amusements and splendid decorations—not to mention the hundreds of millions sunk by intemperance, and swallowed up in the deep dark vortex of infamous dissipation! Men are lavish of money on objects on which their hearts are set. And if the hearts of Christians *were set* on saving the heathen, as much as wicked men are set on their pleasures, would they, think you, be content with the present measure of their contributions?

Look, too, at what men can do who are eager in the pursuit of wealth. Under the [Pg 77] influence of such an incentive, railroads, canals, and fortresses spring into being, and fleets bedeck the seas like the stars of the firmament. Money is not wanting when lucrative investment is the end in view. Even professed Christians can collect together heavy sums, when some great enterprise promises a profitable income. They profess, perhaps, to be accumulating money for Christ; but, alas, to what a painful extent does it fail of reaching the benevolent end proposed! Worldly men accomplish much, for their hearts are enlisted. Professed Christians, too, accomplish much in worldly projects, for their minds become engrossed. What then could they not accomplish for Christ, if their feelings were equally enlisted in his cause? They might have, in serving Christ, intellects as vigorous, muscles as strong, and this advantage in addition, a God on high who has vouchsafed to help them.

Take another view of the case. The child that is now sitting by your side in perfect health, is suddenly taken sick. Its blooming cheeks turn pale, and it lifts its languid and imploring eyes for help. You call a physician, the most skillful one you can obtain. [Pg 78]

Do you think of expense? A protracted illness swells the bill of the physician and apothecary to a heavy amount. Do you dismiss the physician, or withhold any comfort for fear of expense?

Your child recovers, and becomes a promising youth. He takes a voyage to a foreign country. The ship is driven from her course, and wrecked on some barbarous coast. Your son becomes a captive, and after long anxiety you hear that he is alive, and learn his suffering condition; and you are told that fifty dollars will procure his ransom. I will suppose you are poor, have not a dollar at command, and that the sum can be raised in no other way than by your own industry and toil. Now, I ask, how many months would expire before you would save the sum from your hard earnings, and liberate your son? But what is an Algerine dungeon? It is a heaven, compared with the condition of the heathen. In the one case, there are bodily sufferings; in the other, present wretchedness and eternal agonies.

I once fell in company with a man of moderate circumstances, with whom I used the above argument. He promptly replied, "It is [Pg 79] true. Three years ago I thought I could barely support my family by my utmost exertions. Two years since, my darling son became deranged, and the support of him at the asylum costs me four hundred dollars a year. I find that with strict economy and vigorous exertion I can meet the expense. But if any one had said to me three years ago, that I could raise four hundred dollars a year to save a lost world, I should have regarded the remark as the height of extravagance."

Now, I ask, ought not men to feel as much in view of the eternal and unspeakable agony of a world of souls, as a parent feels for a suffering child? God felt more. He loved his only Son with a most tender affection—inconceivably more tender than any earthly parent can exercise towards a beloved child. And yet, when the Father placed before him, on the one hand the eternal ruin of men, and on the other the sufferings and death of his beloved Son, which did he choose? Let Gethsemane and Calvary answer. Can Christians then have much of the spirit of God, and not feel for the eternal agonies of untold millions, more than for the temporal sufferings of a beloved child? But if Christians felt thus, [Pg 80] what exertion would they make—how immense the sum they would cheerfully raise, this present year, to evangelize the heathen! Feeling thus, a few of the wealthy churches might sustain the present expenditures of all foreign operations. Yet all the American churches combined, *feeling as they do now*, fail to send forth a few waiting missionaries, and suffer the schools abroad to be disbanded. The truth is, in the scale of giving, the church as a body (I say nothing of individuals or of particular churches) has scarcely risen in its feeling above the freezing point. What they now contribute is a mere fraction compared with their ability.

Millions are squandered by professed Christians on a pampered appetite, in obedience to fashion, a taste for expensive building, a love of parade, and on newly-invented comforts and conveniences, of which the hardy soldiers of Jesus Christ ought ever to be ignorant.

Then, again, some who are economical in their expenditures, have little conception of what is meant by total consecration to God. There must be an entire reform in this matter. Every Christian must feel that his employment, whether it be agriculture, merchandise, [Pg 81] medicine, law, or anything else, is of no value any farther than it is connected with the Redeemer's kingdom; that wealth is trash, and life a trifle, *except* as they may be used to advance the cause of Christ; and that so far as they may be used for this purpose, they are of immense value. Let every Christian feel this sentiment— let it be deeply engraven on his heart, and how long, think you, would pecuniary means be wanting in the work of the world's salvation?

And do we *go and instruct* the heathen as we ought? This is indeed the main point. To pray, formally at least, is quite easy; to give, is a little more difficult; but to go, in the minds of most persons, is entirely out of the question. Satan understood human nature when he said, "All that a man hath will he give for his life." Speak of going, and you touch the man, his skin and his bones. To go, requires that a man have such feelings as to begin to act in earnest, as men do in other matters. Men act in person, when they are deeply in earnest. In the case supposed of a sick child, does the mother simply express a desire that the child may recover? does she merely give money, and hire a nurse to take [Pg 82] little or no care of it? No: in her *own person* she anticipates its every want, with the utmost attention and watchfulness. When a son is in bondage on a barbarous coast, does the father merely *pray* that his son may be redeemed? does he merely send *money* for his ransom? No: he chooses, if possible, *to go in person* and carry the sum, that no means may be left untried to accomplish the object he has so much at heart. Men who are deeply interested in an important matter, where there is much at stake, cannot be satisfied with sending; they choose to *go themselves.* This remark is true in all the enterprises and transactions of life the world over.

If then, after all, the measure of going is the true measure of interest, to what extent, I inquire, have Christians of America gone to the heathen? Alas! the number is few, very few.

Look at the proportion of *ministers* who go abroad. In the United States the number of preachers, of all denominations, is perhaps not far from one to a thousand souls. This is in a land already intelligent and Christian; in a land of universities, colleges, and schools; in a land of enterprise, of industry, and of [Pg 83] free institutions, where the arts flourish, and where improvements are various and unnumbered; and more than all, in a land where more than a million and a half of the people are professed Christians, and ready to aid the ministers of Christ in various ways. On the other hand, even if missionaries from all Christendom be taken into the account, there is not more than one minister to a million of pagan souls, with almost no intelligent Christians to assist as teachers, elders, catechists, and tract distributers; no physicians, artists, and judicious legislators, to improve society and afford the means of civilized habits; no literature worthy of the name; no colleges, or even common schools of any value; no industry and enterprise, and every motive for it crushed by arbitrary and tyrannical institutions: the mind degraded and besotted, inconceivably so, and preoccupied also with the vilest superstition, the most inveterate prejudices, and the most arrogant bigotry. Who can measure the vast disproportion? What mind sufficient to balance extremes so inconceivably immense? On the one hand a minister to a thousand souls, with many helpers and a thousand auxiliary influences in his [Pg 84] favor; on the other, one minister to a million of souls, with no helpers and no auxiliary influences, finding out an untrodden track amidst unnumbered obstacles, and penetrating with his single lamp into the dark and boundless chaos of heathenism. This is the manner in which Christendom shows that she loves her neighbor as herself; and in view of it, judge ye, whether American Christians go as much as they ought to instruct and save the benighted nations.

We said, that the number of missionaries to the heathen population is about one to a million of souls; but let not the conclusion be drawn, that every million of heathen souls has a missionary. By no means. The few hundred missionaries preach to a few hundred thousand souls. The millions and hundreds of millions of heathen, are as destitute of preaching as though a missionary had never sailed, as destitute of the Scriptures as though a Bible were never printed, and as far from salvation, I was about to say, as though Jesus Christ had never died. Men speak of operating upon the *world*. Such language is delusive. The present style of effort, or anything like it, can only operate on some small [Pg 85] portions of the earth. To influence materially the *wide world*, Christians must awake to a style of praying, giving, and *going* too, of which they have as yet scarcely dreamed. The work of going into all the world and preaching the Gospel to every creature, has scarcely been undertaken in earnest. And how vain it would be to expect to make any material impression on the world, as a whole, when so small a company from all the ministers in the United States go abroad, and a less number even of lay members from the vast body of a million and a half.

The heathen are not lost because a Saviour is not provided for them. "God so loved the world that he gave his only begotten Son." The preaching of the cross is "the power of God and the wisdom of God" both to the Jew and the Greek. Facts show, that in every nation, however barbarous and degraded, the Gospel of Jesus has power to convert, purify, elevate and save. These facts are irresistible.

Neither are the heathen lost, because the ocean separating them is rarely passed. For the sake of gain, men can visit the most distant and sultry climes. To solve a question of science or merely to gratify curiosity, [Pg 86] they can circumnavigate the globe, or penetrate far into the icy regions of the poles. The improvements in navigation and the extension of commerce have united the two continents in one. The Atlantic ocean no longer separates you from Africa, nor the Pacific from China. The amount of intercourse between the seekers of wealth from Christian lands and almost every heathen country, is absolutely immense.

Why then are the heathen left to perish? There is a lack of earnestness in the church in the work of the world's conversion. What does the present earnestness of the church amount to? They contribute on an average two cents a month each, and they find that the pittance of money will more than suffice for the small number of men: and then the cry is "More money than men." A few men are obtained and then the pittance of money fails, and "More men than money" is the cry. A year or two afterwards the supply of men is gone, and the cry again is reversed. As if, in repairing the wastes of the New-York fire, the citizens collect together a small quantity of brick, and then find they have more brick than workmen. So they employ [Pg 87] a few more men, and then find they have more men than brick. Was this the rate at which the ravages of the great fire were so soon repaired? Was this the measure of their engagedness in rebuilding the city?

Some derangement takes place in the Erie Canal: a lock fails, an aqueduct gives way, or a bank caves in. Is business stopped on the canal till the next season, because the times are hard, and it is difficult to obtain money to make repairs? Some derangement takes place in a railroad: is travelling postponed till next year? But in the work of doing good, the reverse of times is regarded as a sufficient excuse to detain missionaries, disband schools, and take other retrograde steps. We coolly block our wheels, lie still, and postpone our efforts for the world's conversion till more favorable times. Men are earnest in worldly matters: in digging a canal, in laying a railroad, or in repairing a city; but in God's work — the work of saving the nations — their efforts are so weak that one is at loss to know which is most prominent, the folly, or the enormous guilt.

Is it not a fact, that in our efforts for the heathen we come so far short of our ability, [Pg 88] that God cannot consistently add his blessing. Can it be that the service rendered by the church as a body is acceptable to God? It is not according to that she hath—it forms an immense and inconceivable contrast to that measure of effort which lies fully within her power. Is it not, then, as though an imperfect sacrifice were offered to the Lord—a lamb full of blemish? If the church were weak, and it were really beyond her ability to do more than she does at present, then God would accomplish great victories by the feeble means. He can save by few as well as by many. He would make the "worm Jacob to thresh mountains." But since God has blessed the American church with numbers, and with great and peculiar advantages, he requires of her efforts that accord with her ability. The poor widow's mites accomplish much; but the wealthy man's mites, or the wealthy nation's thousands, when she is fully able to give millions; and her very few sons, when it would even benefit her to spare a host of her ablest men; what shall we say of such an offering? The reason why God blesses the efforts of the American church may be, that there are *some widows*, and some others too [Pg 89] who do what they can—who honestly come up to the measure of their ability. For the sake of these God may add his blessing, just as for the sake of ten righteous men he would have spared Sodom. But no very great and conspicuous blessing can be expected to attend the labors of missionaries, such as the conversion of China, or of Africa, till the church begins to *pray, give* and *go*, according to her *ability*; till she begins to come up to the extent of her powers in her efforts to save the heathen. Then, when she renders according to that she hath, her service will be accepted; it will be a sweet savor before God; his throne of love will come near the tabernacle of his saints, and the noise of his chariot soon be heard among the ranks of the enemy. The church then, with Christ at their head, shall go on rapidly from conquering to conquer, till all nations, tongues and people, shall bow the knee before him. As soon as the church shall put forth all her strength so as to render an acceptable service to God, it is of little consequence whether she be weak or strong, few or many, the blessing will descend; the mountains will break forth into singing, and the trees shall clap their hands [Pg 90] for joy; God will come, take up his abode with the saints, and verify all that is expressed by "the latter day glory."

It is plain, then, not only that Christians come far short of doing what they can to save the heathen, but that if they would come up to the measure of their duty they might, under God, rescue the dying nations from their impending doom. If they would engage in earnest, pray with fervency and faith, and prove their zeal by giving and by going, then the providence of God would not leave a bolt or a bar in their way, except what might be necessary to test their perseverance. Let every ambassador of Christ, and *every Christian too*, possess the unreserved consecration of Paul, and manifest that burning zeal which carried him, as on the wings of an angel, to preach to the Gentiles the unsearchable riches of Christ; let every redeemed sinner, minister or layman, stand ready, not merely to contribute of his substance, but to traverse with cheerful step the burning plains of Africa or the icy mountains of Greenland: then the darkness that now envelopes the earth would soon be dispelled, the torch of Revelation be carried to the most distant lands, and its light [Pg 91] be made to penetrate the most gloomy abodes of men; the radiance of heavenly truth would be poured around the dying bed of every pagan, intelligence now in to us from every quarter, not only of individuals, but of nations converted to God, and the shout of triumph would soon be heard, "The kingdoms of this world have become the kingdom of our Lord."

It seems to be true, therefore, that the heathen are sinking to perdition; and true, also, that we might, under God, be the means of saving them. Shall we not then be found *accountable* for their eternal agonies? O Christian, pause and look at this thought! Look at it deliberately, for we shall be obliged to do so at the judgment day. No one can plead exemption from it, unless he does *what he can* to save the heathen. O my soul, how much blood, how much weeping, wailing and gnashing of teeth, will stand at thy account in the day of judgment!

I appeal to each one of you, examine yourselves in the light of this truth. Call up your prayers, your contributions, and your personal efforts. Compare what you have done with what Jesus did for you. I entreat you, open your ears, and hearts too, to the groans of a [Pg 92] dying world. Listen to the notes which, like the noise of seven thunders, peal after peal, are rolling in upon your shores.

"Hark! what mean those lamentations,
Rolling sadly through the sky?

'Tis the cry of heathen nations,
'Come and help us, or we die!'

"Hear the heathen's sad complaining,
Christians! hear their dying cry;
And, the love of Christ constraining,
Haste to help them, ere they die!"

Yes, reader, haste to help them. Confer not with flesh and blood. Meet all vain excuses with a deaf ear and a determined spirit. Let pity move you, the love of Christ constrain you, and a sense of responsibility urge you, to take that precious Gospel on which your hopes rely, and to carry it, without delay, to the perishing nations. [Pg 93]

CHAPTER IV.

THE SAVIOUR'S LAST COMMAND.

Let us suppose that all kindreds and people of the earth are assembled, and that the inhabitants of Africa, Asia, the Isles of the Pacific and the wilds of America, are called upon to speak, and to give in their testimony *how far the Saviour's last command has been obeyed.*

The inquiry is first put to Africa:

"Africa, to what extent and for what purpose have people from Christian lands visited thee, and thine adjacent islands? What have they carried to thy shores? And what is the treatment thou hast received from them? Tell the whole truth: let it be known to what extent the Saviour's last command has been obeyed in respect to thee."

To this inquiry Africa replies:

"The truth I can tell, but the *whole* truth cannot be told. I have indeed been visited by people from Christian lands. Thousands and hundreds of thousands from those lands [Pg 94] have visited my shores. Some have come to measure the pyramids, and to gather relics of ancient literature and decayed magnificence; some to search out the sources of the Nile and the course of the Niger; some to possess the best of the soil; and a vast multitude have come, with a cruelty that knows no mercy, to tear the husband from his wife and the wife from her husband, parents from their children and children from their parents, brother from sister and sister from brother — to crowd them together without distinction of age or sex in the suffocating holds of their ships, where a large proportion of them die, and to convey the remainder far away to spend their lives in degrading servitude. They have brought beads and trinkets; they have brought *instruments of death*, such as muskets, powder, knives and swords; and they have brought, too, full cargoes of *liquid poison*. The navies of Christian, lands have fought in my harbors, and their armies upon my shores. Their money by millions has been lavished, and their blood has run in torrents.

"A few individuals, however, of a different character, have found their way hither. They have come in the spirit of benevolence and of [Pg 95] peace, and have brought in their hands the precious treasure of the Gospel of Christ. But their number is so small as to be almost lost among the multitude. For one who has taught righteousness, purity, truth and mercy, thousands have taught, by their example, rapacity, drunkenness, lewdness and cruelty. For one who has led us in the path of life, thousands have led us in the paths of destruction. For one who has brought the Bible, thousands have brought rum. For one whose example has been salutary, the intercourse of thousands has left a loathsome disease, which with sure and rapid progress is depopulating the land. Such is the sum of my testimony. Days and nights would be required to give the detail."

This testimony of Africa being finished, the same inquiry is put to Asia:

"Asia, to what extent have the nations of Christendom visited thee, and thy numerous islands? What have they carried to thy shores? and what has been their deportment towards thee?"

To which Asia replies:

"The vast number, either of men or of ships from Christian lands, that have visited [Pg 96] my shores, cannot be told. I know full well the enterprise, the energy, and the perseverance of Christian lands; yes, verily, and traits too of less honorable name. Large portions of my territory acknowledge the control of their armies. Their thundering navies lie in my harbors and sail along my coasts. Ships without number—mighty ships whose masts pierce the clouds, have come for my teas, my crapes, my silks, my spices and other precious merchandise. Their consuls, superintendents, officers of various kinds, and merchants in great numbers, dwell in almost every port, and have erected in those ports stores, shops, offices and sumptuous dwellings. Many things pleasant and useful have been brought hither, but many things also that are ruinous: full cargoes of ardent spirits; and immense quantities of opium too, a means of destruction no less sure.

"Among the multitudes who have come to my shores, some few, indeed, have brought the Gospel of Christ, made known its truths and exemplified its spirit; but the thousands and tens of thousands have inculcated by their example, worldliness, drunkenness, lewdness, war, violence and treachery. If needful, a [Pg 97] volume of details might be given; but this is the sum."

Next, the inquiry is put to the Isles of the Ocean:

"Great Pacific, to what extent has the last command of Christ been obeyed by Christian lands, in respect to thy numerous islands?"

The reply is as follows:

"Thousands of ships from Christian lands continually cruise upon my wide waters, and visit my numerous groups of islands. They have exchanged with my ignorant and destitute inhabitants, beads, trinkets, and a few inches of rusty iron hoop, for the best produce of the islands. They have sold to them guns, powder and rum. Many of their ships have been floating grog-shops—floating exhibitions too of Sodom and Gomorrah. From some, on slight provocation, broadsides of cannon have been fired on my heedless inhabitants, strewing the deep with the dead and the dying. Rum and disease have been introduced. The one has slain its thousands, and the other has slain, and is still slaying its tens of thousands. Many useful things indeed have been introduced, but in connection with a host of evils! A few individuals too, bear [Pg 98] ing the Gospel of Jesus Christ, have visited some of my numerous islands; but what are they among the multitude?"

After this testimony of the Isles of the Ocean, the inquiry is last addressed to America:

"America, what is thy testimony? From Bhering's Straits to Cape Horn, what treatment have thy native inhabitants received from Christian nations?"

America replies:

"Alas! scarcely enough remain of my miserable inhabitants to return an answer. They have been swept away by the same causes which are now sweeping away the inhabitants of the Pacific. The rapacity of those called Christians, which has not scrupled at any means of conquest and extirpation, and the rum and diseases introduced, have laid my numerous population in the grave. Have I been visited by those who bear the Christian name? Yes, verily, they now possess the best portions of my territory, and have grown into vast nations on my soil. Even my veriest wilds have been repeatedly traversed by them in search of furs; and the tracks they have made been too often marked with drunk [Pg 99] enness, lewdness, and treachery. Few, very few indeed of all that have come to this vast continent, have come to instruct my ignorant inhabitants in the precious Gospel of Jesus Christ, and lead them in the paths of righteousness and peace. Few who explore my wilds, explore them for this purpose. Alas! a far different object prompts their enterprise, their energy, and their perseverance. This is the sum of my testimony."

Now, reader, let us look well at this testimony of Africa, of Asia, of the Isles of the Ocean, and of America. Is it not overwhelming? Take, the Encyclopedia of Geography, or McCulloch's Dictionary of Commerce, or Howitt's Colonization and Christianity, and carefully examine the facts. Are they not enough to strike us dumb? To what a vast extent heathen nations have been visited by those who bear the Christian name. What obscure island, or what obscure nook or corner of the earth has not been visited? What immense multitudes have gone forth. And, alas! for what purposes. How few, how very few have gone forth to make known the Gospel! What a powerful motive among men is the love of earthly gain, and how [Pg 100] weak a motive is love to Christ and regard to his last command. The command reads, "Go ye into all the world and preach the gospel to every creature." Christian nations, ye have not failed in great multitudes to "go into all the world;" scarcely have ye failed to visit "every creature;" but for what purpose have ye gone forth? Has it been mainly to make known the precious name of Jesus? Be entreated to look at the case as it is, for a day of impartial retribution is at hand.

Many of you indeed, who go forth to heathen shores, do not profess to be the disciples of Jesus; but imagine not, that on that account your guilt is diminished. Ye who reject the Saviour, and disobey his commands—who throw away your own souls as worthless, and are reckless of the souls of your fellow men, what can you say in the day of Christ's appearing? If ye had only destroyed your own souls, then your case would be more tolerable; but since you withhold from the millions of ignorant heathen the knowledge of salvation, which has been imparted to you—not only refusing to enter the kingdom of heaven yourselves, but deny [Pg 101] ing the key to those who might be disposed to enter;—and not only do this, but in your intercourse with the heathen, which has been very abundant, confirm them in their evil practices by a pernicious example, and hurry them by thousands to the grave by means of *deadly poison* and *deadly disease*—Oh! how will you endure the keen remorse and fearful looking for of judgment, which may ere long overtake you? When the impartial Judge shall appear, and your eyes shall meet his eye, what agonies must rend your souls!

But some of you have the vows of God upon you. To such I would say, Be entreated to look at the case as it is. As ye have gone forth on voyages of just and honorable traffic, and on voyages of discovery, have you manifested in all the heathen ports where you touched, that to make known the Saviour was the great and absorbing desire of your hearts? Alas! are there not some among you who, either as owners, masters or agents, are connected with ships that

54

sail from port on the Sabbath, or do other unnecessary work on that day, and who thereby teach the heathen, wherever those ships go, to disobey God when their gain or convenience require it? Are [Pg 102] there not also some among you, who, in one way or another, are connected with ships whose outfits are wholly or in part, beads, trinkets, guns, powder, rum and opium? and who thereby teach the heathen injustice, cheating, drunkenness, lewdness, and recklessness of life? Why is it that ye bear the name of the peaceful disciples of the benevolent Jesus, whilst ye are concerned in scattering among the heathen "fire-brands, arrows and death" — in teaching them every species of iniquity, and in rearing a wall of prejudice strong and high to the progress of the Gospel?

But most of my readers stand pure from all this crime; and of such I simply inquire, with deep concern and affectionate earnestness, Why, dear brethren, have ye not obeyed the Saviour's last command? Why have ye not made known the Gospel of Christ to every creature? Each one of you has doubtless some excuse at hand, or he could not escape the goadings of conscience. Let us then, in the spirit of candor and honesty, look at some excuses.

Perhaps some one may be inclined to say, "The work enjoined by the Saviour's last [Pg 103] command is a very great work, and there has not been time enough to perform it."

True, I reply, the work is great; but how does it appear that there has not been sufficient time to accomplish it? *Not sufficient time!* What has been accomplished in the pursuit of wealth and honor during the same period of time? What has been done at home in railroads, canals, steamboats, manufactures, and in other departments of enterprise and industry? What has been done abroad? Look at the testimony of Africa, Asia, the Isles of the Pacific, and the wilds of America. There has been time to carry rum to every shore. There has been time to introduce diseases among every barbarous people, which are hurrying them to the grave by thousands. There has been time to kidnap thousands and hundreds of thousands of the degraded Africans. There has been time to extirpate most of the native population of North and South America. There has been time to wage war, till the blood of human beings has flowed in torrents. And then, in regard to just and honorable traffic, compute, if human arithmetic be competent to the task, the amount of merchandise brought from [Pg 104] India, and from other distant lands. There has been time for all this. Now I ask with great plainness, for it is a solemn and practical subject, Had you exhibited the same enterprise, energy and perseverance, in making known the Gospel to all nations, as has been exhibited in worldly pursuits, would not every human being, long ere this, have heard the word of life? Will you not, Christian reader, look at this question, weigh it well, and deal honestly with your own soul?

Here, I am suspicious that some may be inclined to excuse themselves with a vague thought secretly entertained, which, if expressed, would be somewhat as follows:

"True, we have not exhibited as much zeal in teaching all nations as has been exhibited by the worldly, and by many of ourselves even, in the pursuit of wealth. But we claim not the praise of a holy, self-denying and apostolic life. We are content with an *humble* walk in the Christian course, and a *low* seat in heaven. Entire consecration, in the sense urged, is what we never *professed*."

Your standard, then, it appears is very low — too low, it may be, to admit you even to that humble seat in the courts above which you [Pg 105] anticipate. You claim not the praise of an apostolic life, and I seriously fear that you will not obtain even the testimony of being a true Christian. But how does it appear, that you never professed an entire consecration to Christ of all your powers of body and soul? It is true, the conduct of some would seem to say, that they put on a form of religion to silence their fears, to cheat themselves with a delusive hope, and to enjoy a comfortable state of mind on earth. But what, really, are the vows that rest upon you? What else than to seek by prayer and effort, as your supreme aim, chief desire, and all-engrossing object, the promotion of Christ's kingdom — the salvation of souls for whom he died?

Besides, what is the great purpose for which the church was instituted? Certainly, not to promote in its members a delusive comfort and quietude of mind; neither mainly nor chiefly to secure their own ultimate salvation; but *to take advantage of union of strength to convert the world.* The church — the whole church, without the exception of any of its members, is by profession, not merely a missionary society, but a *missionary band:* the minute-men of the Lord Jesus, ready to do [Pg 106] his will, at home or abroad, with singleness of aim, and with a spirit of entire devotion.

"But," you say, "were we thus to live, the world would verily believe we were deranged."

Deranged! it would be the right kind of derangement. Were not the apostles thought to be deranged? And the Reformers—Luther, Melancthon, Calvin, Knox and others—were not they thought to be enthusiasts and zealots? Why? Because they were somewhat in earnest in the cause of Christ. Worldly men toil and strive night and day, in collecting together a little of the pelf and dust of the earth, and think themselves wise in doing so; but if the disciples of Christ show zeal or earnestness, in pursuits as much higher than theirs as heaven is higher than the earth, and as much more important as the immortal soul is more valuable than corruption and vanity, they call them enthusiasts and fanatics! But, alas! how few of us who profess to be the disciples of Christ, have manifested such zeal in his service as to be called by such epithets. Such persons alone God calls wise; and those worldly men, who are mad in the pursuit of wealth, God calls "fools." The wisdom of God and the wis [Pg 107] dom of the world are utterly at variance. O that all who profess to love Christ, manifested such zeal in obeying him as to be strange and singular men! How soon would every human being hear his Gospel! But since such zeal is not manifested, the heathen are left to perish; and where, I ask affectionately and solemnly, where rests the guilt?

But, here it may perhaps be replied, "Our sin is a sin of ignorance. We have not been acquainted with the full import of the Saviour's last command, nor with the extent of our obligations to Christ. Neither have we been acquainted with the wretched and guilty condition of the heathen world, nor with the exertions necessary to turn it from darkness to light, from the power of Satan unto God. God will wink at our sin, if we be indeed guilty, for we have not been enlightened on this subject."

I answer. Does ignorance of the laws of any nation excuse those who transgress those laws; or is it not considered to be the duty of all subjects to inform themselves in respect to the laws of their country? And should it not be so in the kingdom of Christ? The requirements of Christ in their full extent are con [Pg 108] tained in the New Testament, and are expressed in language that need not be misunderstood. If any one has mistaken their import, is it not on account of a self-seeking, money-getting, or slothful disposition? Let such a one search his own heart, and inquire with concern, "Did I desire to know my duty? Was not my blindness a matter of choice; no infirmity, no misfortune, but my guilt? If there had been a desire, nay, even a willingness to be instructed, could I have mistaken such plain and unequivocal precepts of the Gospel?"

The condition too of the heathen, their guilty and wretched condition, is fully made known in the New Testament, especially in the first chapter of Paul's epistle to the Romans. Besides, accounts of their guilt and wretchedness have been presented before the Christian community in Heralds, Chronicles, reports and newspapers, till they have become too familiar to make an impression. Can ignorance at this day be any other than a criminal ignorance—an ignorance of fearful responsibility?

And, I ask again, Can it be an excuse to many Christians that they are laymen and [Pg 109] not preachers of the Gospel? Can they make it appear that many of their number were not called to the office of preaching the Gospel? Did they take the proper means to ascertain that point? How, I anxiously inquire, did such persons determine so readily, when a world was sinking to perdition for want of preachers of the Gospel, that they were called to be lawyers, physicians, statesmen, merchants, farmers and manufacturers? Can it be fairly shown that hundreds of laymen have not rejected an office to which they were *called*— solemnly called, by the woes and dying groans of six hundred millions of their fellow men? Is there not reason to fear, that it was from a carnal choice and selfish inclination, rather than a sense of duty, that so great a majority slid so easily into their present occupations?

Besides, how does it appear that only preachers of the Gospel are required to labor directly for the destitute at home, and to go forth to the heathen abroad? It was far otherwise in the days of the apostles. Then the whole church—driven out, indeed, by persecution— went everywhere making known the Saviour. And at the present hour, not only [Pg 110] are ministers needed in propagating the

Gospel in destitute places at home, and in raising up heathen nations from their deep degradation, but there are needed also, in their appropriate spheres, teachers, physicians, mechanics, farmers — in short, men of every useful profession and employment.

Besides, much is to be done at home in sustaining those who go abroad. Has there been no lack in this part of the work? Alas! there are facts to meet such an inquiry, facts too well known to be named: disbanded schools, detained missionaries, and deserted monthly concerts: facts that stand registered on a book that shall hereafter be opened. Dear brethren, I speak earnestly and boldly of your obligations, not forgetting my own; and I would entreat you, by all that is affecting in the death of souls, and by all that is constraining in the love of Christ, to admit freely to your hearts, without subterfuge or excuse, the full import of the Saviour's last command, and to commence at once a life of sincere obedience. O! let us deal *honestly* with ourselves, in a matter of such immense moment.

[Pg 111]

CHAPTER V.

LAYMEN CALLED TO THE FIELD OF MISSIONS.

In Acts, 8:4, it is said, *Therefore they that were scattered abroad, went everywhere preaching the word.* And from the previous verses it seems that these persons, who were scattered abroad, were lay members of the church. The history is instructive.

After the day of Pentecost, the number of converts to Christianity amounted to several thousands. They were Jews, and had strong feelings of attachment to the city of Jerusalem, to the temple, and to the land of their fathers. They therefore clung to Jerusalem, and

seemed inclined to remain together as one large church. But it was
the design of the Lord Jesus, that the Gospel should be preached
everywhere: such was his last and most solemn command. As, therefore, the disciples seemed in a measure unmindful of this command,
the Saviour permitted a persecution to rage, which scattered them
abroad, and they went "everywhere preaching the word." The [Pg
112] term *preaching*, in this place, means simply announcing or making known the news of salvation. This must be the meaning, for
they that were scattered abroad were laymen. As they went, they
told everywhere of Jesus Christ, and of the life and immortality
which he had brought to light. This subject engrossed their
thoughts; their hearts were full of it, and out of the abundance of
their hearts their mouths spake. It is clear from this history, that in
early times lay members of the church, in great numbers, were led,
in the providence of God, to go forth and engage personally in the
work of propagating the Gospel. And the more closely we look at
the history, the more we shall be impressed with this fact.

Notice the *time* chosen by God for the first remarkable outpouring
of his Holy Spirit. It was on the day of Pentecost, when multitudes
were present, not only from all parts of Palestine, but from the surrounding nations. There were present, "Parthians, and Medes, and
Elamites, and the dwellers in Mesopotamia, and in Judea, and Cap-
padocia, in Pontus and Asia, Phrygia and Pamphylia, in Egypt and
the parts of Lybia about Cyrene, [Pg 113] and strangers of Rome,
Jews and proselytes, Cretes and Arabians." Upon this multitude,
assembled from all the nations round about, the Holy Ghost was
poured out with such power, that three thousand souls were converted in one day; and on succeeding days many were added to the
church. Many of these converts would naturally return to the different nations and places from which they came, and make known the
Saviour far and wide. It was by the return of these converts to their
places of residence, that the Gospel was early introduced into many
places quite remote from Jerusalem, among which may be reck-
oned, in all probability, the distant city of Rome. The first propagation of the Gospel in that metropolis of the world, can be traced to
no other source with so much probability, as to the strangers from
Rome who were present at Jerusalem on the day of Pentecost. It
seems evident, therefore, that in the time chosen by God for this

remarkable outpouring of his Spirit, he had an eye to an extensive and rapid propagation of the Gospel by lay members of the church.

Again, as hinted before, when the great body of the first converts chose to remain at [Pg 114] Jerusalem, God saw best to *drive them thence by persecution.* This persecution began with the stoning of Stephen, and raged with such violence, that it is said that all the church at Jerusalem were scattered abroad, except the apostles. They were not only a few individuals who were driven out, but so many as to justify the expression, "all the church." By thus dispersing the great body of the church, the Saviour propagated rapidly and extensively his precious Gospel. For this multitude of lay members — and there were several thousands of them — went everywhere preaching the word; announcing in all places, in a way appropriate to their station, the news of salvation through a crucified Redeemer. They propagated the Gospel throughout Judea and Samaria; and some of them travelled as far as Ph[oe]nice and Cyprus, and laid the foundation of the church at Antioch. It was not till the apostles had heard of the success of these lay members at Antioch, that they sent thither Barnabas to help in the work. It appears, then, that the rapid and extensive propagation of the Gospel, in early times, was accomplished in a great measure by the spreading abroad of the great body of the church; [Pg 115] by an actual going forth and personal engagement of a great multitude of lay members.

Again, the treasurer of Candace, Queen of Ethiopia, seems to have been converted on his return home, not simply out of regard to his own personal salvation, but as a means of making known the Gospel in the distant place of his residence; for soon after, we find in that region a flourishing church of Christ.

Again, look at the example of Aquila and Priscilla, who labored zealously at Corinth and at Ephesus. Look, too, at the whole list of Paul's fellow travellers, and those whom he salutes in his letters as helpers in the Gospel.

From all these facts it is evident, that in early times God made use of common Christians in propagating the Gospel. Did he not so overrule events in his providence, as to show it to be his design that lay members of the church should go forth in great numbers, and engage personally, in ways appropriate and proper for them, in the work of making known Christ? We have then the force of primitive example—of primitive example, too, brought about by the manifest overrulings of God's providence. This example is not equi [Pg 116] valent, indeed, to a "Thus saith the Lord;" yet does it not strongly favor the sentiment, that lay members of the church in great numbers are called to go forth and assist in evangelizing the heathen?

To elevate all nations requires a great variety of laborers. In illustrating this point, I cannot expect to present it with all the clearness and force which are due to it. To appreciate fully its truth and its weighty import, it is necessary to live in the midst of a heathen people, and actually to witness the great variety and amount of labor which must be put forth, in order to elevate and improve them. The work of raising up a people from barbarism to Christianity is not only an immense work, but emphatically a *various* work—a work which requires a great diversity both of means and of laborers. The minister of the Gospel must perform a prominent part, but he must not be expected to labor alone. His unaided efforts are altogether insufficient for the task.

There is special need of other laborers, since the number of ministers among the heathen is likely to be so small; but the need would exist, even though the number of min [Pg 117] isters were very much increased. Labors analogous, both in respect to measure and variety, to those bestowed upon a Christian congregation, must be expended on a congregation of heathen. In Christian countries, a thousand important labors are performed by intelligent and praying men and women in the church, as direct aid to the minister in his arduous work; and a thousand offices are performed by schoolmasters, physicians, lawyers, merchants, farmers, mechanics and artisans, which, though in most cases not aimed directly at the salvation of men, are, notwithstanding, most intimately connected with the world's improvement and renovation. But while ministers at home are assisted in their work, shall the missionary abroad receive little or no help in his direct labors? And in respect to all improvements in society indirectly connected with his main work, must the task of introducing them and of urging them on, devolve entirely on him alone? Why should not the various means of civilizing and improving society at home, be brought to exert their influence upon the heathen abroad? Why should not the aid enjoyed by the minister in Christian lands, from intelligent members of [Pg 118] his church, be afforded to the missionary among the heathen? How, indeed, shall the world be converted, unless there be a going forth to heathen lands from among all classes of Christians?

But I fear that these remarks are too general to be distinctly understood. To make my meaning, then, a little more clear, I will suppose a case.

A missionary goes forth to a barbarous nation, and locates himself in a village of four thousand souls. He learns the language of the people, and soon succeeds in giving them a superficial knowledge of the great truths of the Gospel. God blesses his labors. The people throw away their idols; many sincerely embrace the Lord Jesus; and the community at large acknowledge Christianity as the religion of the land.

Now, a superficial thinker might imagine that the work of elevating the people was almost done; but, in truth, it is but just commenced. The missionary looks upon his people, and wishes them not only to be Christians in name, but to exhibit also intelligence and good order, purity and loveliness, industry and enterprise; in a word, a deportment in [Pg 119] all respects consistent with the religion of Jesus. But what is their state? The government is despotic, and the principles of its administration at variance with Scripture and reason. This takes away all motives to industry and thrift. Then again, the people are ignorant; have no mental discipline, no store of useful knowledge, but their minds are marked with torpor, imbecility, and poverty of thought: while at the same time they are full of grovelling ideas, false opinions, and superstitious notions, imbibed in childhood and confirmed by age. The children, too, are growing up in ignorance of all that is useful and praiseworthy. Entirely uninstructed and ungoverned by their parents; they range at large like the wild goats of the field. The people know not the simple business of making cloth, of working iron, or of framing wood; and have but a very imperfect knowledge of agriculture.

Of course, men, women and children, are almost houseless and naked—destitute of everything but the rudest structures, the rudest fabrications, and the rudest tools and implements of husbandry. A large family herd together, of all ages and both sexes, in [Pg 120] one little hut, sleep on one mat, and eat from one dish. From irregularity of habits and frequent exposure, they are often sick; and with the aid of a superstitious quackery, sink rapidly and in great numbers to the grave.

The missionary looks upon his four thousand villagers, though nominally Christian perhaps, yet still in this state of destitution, degradation and ignorance. He sees, that to elevate them requires the labors not only of a preacher of the Gospel, but the labors of the civilian, the physician, the teacher, the agriculturist, the manufacturer, the mechanic and the artist. Can all these professions and employments be united in one man? Can one missionary sustain all this variety of labor? Yet all these departments of labor are absolutely indispensable to the improvement and elevation of society. They are necessary in a land already Christian. Still more indispensable are they in the work of raising up a people from barbarism.

Teachers are needed. To raise a people from barbarism, the simple but efficient means of common schools must be everywhere diffused; and higher schools too must be established, and vigorously conducted. To teach [Pg 121] the hundreds of millions of adult heathen in week-day schools and in Sabbath-schools, and more especially to instruct and train the hundreds of millions of heathen children and youth, cannot be done by a few hands. We forbear to make a numerical estimate: any one may estimate for himself. The number must be great, even though we look upon them rather as a commencing capital than as an adequate supply, and expect that by far the greater part of laborers are to be trained up from among the heathen themselves. It is preposterous to think of imposing all this labor on a few ministers of the Gospel.

Physicians are needed. They are needed to benefit the bodies of the heathen; for disease, the fruit of sin, is depopulating with amazing speed a large portion of the heathen world. The nations, many of them at least, are melting away. Let physicians go forth, and while they seek to stay the tide of desolation which is sweeping away the bodies of the heathen, let them improve the numerous and very favorable opportunities afforded them of benefiting their souls. The benevolent, sympathizing, and compassionate spirit of Christ, led him to relieve the temporal suffer [Pg 122] ings of men, while his main aim was to secure their eternal salvation. Unless we show, by our exertions, a desire to mitigate the present woes and miseries of men, how shall we convince them that we truly seek their eternal welfare? Physicians must throw their skill in the healing art at the feet of the Saviour, and be ready to use it when and where he shall direct. The number who should go to the heathen cannot, and need not, be named.

It is unnecessary to remark that *printers*, *book-binders*, and *book-distributers* are needed to carry on the work of the world's conversion.

Civilians too are needed: men skilled in laying the foundation of nations and guiding their political economy. Should such men go forth, and evince by a prayerful, godly, and disinterested deportment and course of procedure, that their sole aim was to promote the happiness of the people, both temporal and eternal; there are many barbarous countries where they would readily acquire much influence, and be able in a gradual manner, by friendly and prudent suggestions to the rulers, and in other ways, to effect changes that would be productive of incalculable good. Many changes, with pains-taking and care, [Pg 123] could be made to appear to the rulers to be really for their interest, as well as for the interest of the people; and more light and knowledge, without the intervention of any new motive, would soon introduce them.

A few years since, the king and chiefs of the Sandwich Islands sent a united appeal to the United States for such an instructor, to guide them in the government of their kingdom, and offered him a competent support. While the nation had improved in religion and morals, the government had remained much as it was—keeping the people in the condition of serfs. The system was wrong throughout: of the very worst kind, both for the interests of the rulers and of the subjects. The chiefs began to see this, and asked for an instructor. Such an instructor was not obtained; and one of the missionaries was constrained, by the urgent necessity, to leave the service of the mission board, and to become a political teacher to the king and chiefs. His efforts have been crowned with great success.

Civilians might do good also, not only in the way of their profession, but by a Christian example, and by instructing the people, as [Pg 124] opportunity should offer, in the knowledge of Christ.

Commercial men also, actuated by the same benevolent and disinterested spirit, might develope the resources of heathen lands, and apply them in a wise manner for the benefit of those lands; promote industry, and afford the means of civilized habits; increase knowledge, by expediting communication; and in this way, indirectly, though efficiently, aid the progress of the Gospel. By exhibiting also in their dealings an example of honesty, uprightness, and a conscientious regard to justice and truth; by showing practically the only proper use of wealth, the good of men and the glory of God; by conversing daily with individuals, as did Harlan Page and Normand Smith, at their houses and by the wayside, on the great subject of the soul's salvation; and by presenting in themselves and in their families examples of a prayerful and godly life, they might exert a powerful influence, and perform a very important part in Christianizing the world.

There is also much need of farmers, mechanics, manufacturers and artisans. They should go forth like other laborers in the field, [Pg 125] *not with the selfish design of enriching themselves*, but with the disinterested intention of benefiting the nations. Private gain must be kept strictly, carefully, and absolutely *subordinate*, or immense evil will be wrought and no good be done. They should be men who cheerfully throw themselves and their property on the altar of *entire consecration*, and go forth to labor and toil so long as the Saviour pleases to employ them, with the *lofty design* of doing good to the bodies and souls of their perishing fellow men. Going forth with such a spirit, and with emphasis I repeat, allowing *no other* to intrude, they could do much in raising up the nations from their deep degradation. In the first place, they could do much good by communicating a knowledge of their several employments. Not only is a reform in government necessary, but an introduction of the useful arts also, to raise up the people from their indolence and filthy habits, and to promote thrift, order, neatness and consistency. Look at a heathen family as above described. How can you expect from them refinement or elevation of soul? How can you expect from them the proprieties and consistencies of a Christian life? Even though [Pg

126] they may attend the sanctuary, and be instructed in schools; and even though the government be reformed, and hold out motives to industry; yet will not something else be wanting? Unless the various useful arts and occupations be introduced, how is the land to be filled with fruitful fields, pleasant dwellings, and neatly clad inhabitants? And to introduce these improvements, *men must go forth for the purpose.* Such men too might do good, by exhibiting in themselves and in their families habits of industry, domestic peace and strict economy; by holding up the hands of Christ's ministers, and by scattering the word of life in their appropriate spheres.

That laymen of every useful occupation are needed in heathen lands, is by no means the opinion of one alone. In looking over the periodicals and papers of the last few years, I find that such is the sober and deliberate opinion of many foreign laborers. I find urgent appeals for such helpers from at least five important missionary fields. Would such appeals be made if the enterprise were not a feasible one?

Look too at the fact, that *there is scarcely a nation on the globe where men do not go, [Pg 127] and permanently reside for the purpose of making money.* It is absolutely amazing to what an extent this is the truth. Why then cannot men go forth, and while they obtain a livelihood, make it their ultimate and chief aim to do good?

But the inquiry arises, In what way should laymen go forth? It may not be desirable that they should go forth, to any great extent, under the care of missionary boards at present existing, lest the objects of those boards should become too numerous and complicated. And it may not perhaps be desirable, or necessary, to have any other organization for the purpose. I am not wise enough to give an opinion; but would suggest, that men of some pecuniary means take those means, and emigrate to heathen lands, just as some good men have gone to the far West. May there not also be small combinations of men, not to help others, but *each other* into the field, just as there is in worldly enterprise? When once established in the field, it is supposed that their trades and occupations will afford them, with trials, hardships and reverses, an adequate subsistence, and open before them a wide door of usefulness. [Pg 128]

Some have suggested, that ministers of the Gospel should go forth and sustain themselves abroad. That is a far different question. If ministers of the Gospel ought not to sustain themselves in Christian countries by laboring with their hands, still less should they attempt such a course in foreign fields. They have *other work* to do — enough to occupy all their time.

But for laymen to go forth, and sustain themselves in this way, is it not both proper and appropriate? and have not such enterprises, to some extent, been already entered upon with success? Different fields, of course, present greater or less obstacles; but what undertaking is without its difficulties? Perplexities, embarrassments and sufferings, would be a matter of course; but no greater and perhaps far less than those Christians endured, who, being scattered abroad from their beloved Jerusalem, went everywhere preaching the word.

It may perhaps be objected, that should many from all classes of Christians thus go forth, to live and labor abroad, they would soon possess the land, while the heathen would melt away before them. Let us look at this point. And first, where is the evi [Pg 129] dence of such a result? When and where has the experiment been tried to justify such a supposition? When and where have individuals or companies gone forth with the sole design of benefiting the heathen, and yet proved their extermination? The settlers of New England are not an example in point, for the improvement and salvation of the heathen was not their main aim. It was indeed an idea in mind, but not fully and prominently carried out. It is *yet to be proved* that a company of persons, however numerous, of disinterested views, aiming solely to save the nations, and directing all their energies of body and of mind to that end, would prove the extermination of the heathen, instead of their salvation.

Neither can it be presumed that the descendants of such persons, trained, as ought to be supposed, with faith and prayer, would possess a spirit so selfish and different from that of their fathers, as to prove the extermination of the heathen. And if such is the necessary event, what is the conclusion at which we must arrive? It seems certain, that a mere handful of missionaries cannot put forth the instrumentality which, according to God's usual providence, is necessary to [Pg 130] save them: that a great number and variety of laborers are needed to do the work. Let us be slow, therefore, to trust in the objection; for if it must be admitted, the lawful inference will not necessarily be, that Christians of all classes and in great numbers should not go forth to the heathen; but the inquiry will arise, whether heathen nations as nations must not cease to exist, and remnants of them only be saved—a painful and dread alternative, from which every benevolent heart must instinctively recoil.

There are other reasons why laymen should engage in the work of missions. The work of the world's conversion is too great, too momentous and too pressing, to admit of exemption simply on the ground of profession or employment. When the liberties of a people are at stake, how few are excused from the field of battle? But now the question is not one of temporal liberty: it is whether six hundred millions of the human race shall be won to the company of the redeemed on high, or left to sink in the untold agonies of the world of woe. In this unparalleled emergency, when the question is, whether the destiny of a world shall be heaven or hell, who [Pg 131] can be excused on so slight a ground as that of profession or employment? A few ministers cannot do the work. It is too great. It is presumptuous to expect, that a speedy and complete triumph is to be effected by a few missionaries of the right stamp going through the length and breadth of Satan's extensive and dark empire, and sounding as they go the trumpet of the Gospel around his strong fortifications and deep intrenchments. Such an expectation places an immeasurable disparity between the means and the end. It supposes it to be so easy to effect a transformation of heathen society, heathen habits, heathen minds, and heathen character, and to raise them up from a degradation many ages deep, that a few sounds only from the herald of salvation, as he passes on his way, are sufficient. "Leviathan is not thus tamed." The prince of the power of the air is not thus vanquished.

Neither can the work be effected by a small number of preachers, stationed at different posts, in the midst of the wide domains of darkness and death. Like specks of light, few and far between, how can they illumine the broad canopy of darkness? To commit [Pg 132] the work of the world's conversion to a few missionaries is, in effect, to leave the heathen to perish. A large company of preachers must go forth, and a large company too of other laborers. There must be among the whole body of Christians, not only an interest in the work, but to a greater extent than is imagined, *a personal enlistment*—an actual going forth to foreign lands.

Again, laymen must go abroad; for no less a movement than this will convince them that the work of saving the heathen presses upon them individually, and with all its weight and responsibility. Mere giving does not seem to answer the purpose. Very few laymen at home seem to imagine that they, individually, are as responsible for the life and death of the heathen, as the laborers abroad. Many seem to act only as they are acted upon. This *passive* state will not answer: there must be a more general feeling of personal responsibility. And how is such a feeling of equal and individual responsibility to be induced, till laymen in great numbers begin to go abroad? Till then, there will be a spirit of luxury in the church; a spirit of worldly-mindedness, and a spirit of commit [Pg 133] ting the world's conversion to other hands. To destroy this spirit, which is evidently eating out the piety of the churches, laymen must be urged to arise; to break off their luxuries, to bury their covetousness—to make an entire devotement of body, soul and spirit, to the *direct* and arduous work of saving the heathen.

Once, I remember, after urging laymen to go forth, and to assist in evangelizing the heathen, a father in the church said to me, "Your reasons are just and weighty, but it is of no use to present them before the churches: they have not *piety* enough to act upon them. If you can clearly show that men can accumulate wealth, that they can really make fortunes by going to heathen lands, then your appeals will succeed. Bring this selfish principle to operate, and colonies will quickly scatter over the world. But to go forth with a spirit of self-denial, running the risk of trials and straitened circumstances, and with merely the prospect at best of obtaining a comfortable livelihood and doing good, is a measure not adapted to the present standard of piety in the churches. Until the spirit of devotedness shall rise many degrees in the churches, the [Pg 134] course you urge will be looked upon as entirely visionary."

Alas! can the church be so low in grace? If it be a fact, it is painful and humiliating. If it be true, then the church is lacking in the most essential qualification required of it—is unfitted for the main design of its organization; and is there not reason to fear that God may cast it away, as he has the Roman church, and raise up another after his own heart, that shall do all his pleasure? Christian reader, can you calmly entertain the thought of being set aside by the Lord as unworthy of his employment—of being rejected on the ground of not fulfilling the purpose for which you were called?

CHAPTER VI.

CLAIM OF MISSIONS ON MINISTERS OF INFLUENCE.

In early days, ministers of the greatest influence were called to the work of missions. To prove this assertion, let us read the first verse of the 13th chapter of the Acts of the [Pg 135] Apostles. "Now there were in the church that was at Antioch, certain prophets and teachers; as Barnabas, and Simeon that was called Niger, and Lucius of Cyrene, and Manaen, which had been brought up with Herod the tetrarch, and Saul. As they ministered to the Lord, and fasted, the Holy Ghost said, Separate me Barnabas and Saul, for the work whereunto I have called them." Paul had been at Antioch a whole year, and Barnabas a still longer time. Their labors there had been blessed. The word had been attended with the demonstration of the Spirit and with power, and many people had turned to the Lord, so that a large church had been gathered in that great and opulent city. Believers there became so conspicuous for their numbers, as to be designated by a particular name: "The disciples were called Christians first in Antioch."

There were laboring in that city, besides Paul and Barnabas, three other ministers; "Simeon that was called Niger, and Lucius of Cyrene, and Manaen, who had been brought up with Herod the tetrarch." The Holy Ghost saw that this city, though very important for its numbers, wealth and enterprise, [Pg 136] could not claim the labors of five ministers, while the world at large was entirely destitute of the Gospel. Therefore, on a certain occasion, when the church were worshipping before the Lord and fasting, the Holy Ghost said, "Separate me Barnabas and Saul, for the work whereunto I have called them."

The Holy Ghost did not say, "Separate me Simeon, and Lucius, and Manaen," but, "Separate me Barnabas and Saul"—the spiritual fathers, and main pillars of the church. Had the church been allowed to vote, it doubtless would have spared its sons, rather than its fathers: they would have stated their fond attachment to their first instructors; would have plead the great influence of these two fathers in the church, and the irreparable injury which would be sustained by their leaving it; and would have said, If we must part with some of our teachers, take Simeon, and Lucius, and Manaen, but bereave us not of our spiritual fathers. The question however was not left to their decision. The demand is stern and solemn from the Holy Spirit, with whom there is no selfish bias, "Separate me Barnabas and Saul."

In reflecting on this narration, do we not [Pg 137] come to the conclusion, that men of talents and influence are called to the work of missions?

If this sentiment be true, it is one of immense and practical importance; one that not only ministers, but churches also ought fully to understand. Let us, then, dwell a moment longer on the practice of early times.

The instance to which we have alluded is a striking one; it contains, distinctly and impressively uttered, the mind of the Holy Spirit. It is infallible authority that speaks, and what does it declare? The paramount claim of missions to the ablest, holiest, and most experienced men. If Antioch was required to spare her two ablest men, what may not be required of such cities as Boston, New York, Philadelphia, and Baltimore? And judging too from this case of Antioch, what is the mind of the Holy Ghost in regard to the twelve thousand or more evangelical ministers in the United States? Can it be his will that they should all quietly remain where they are?

Again, God in early times made known his mind on this point, not only by the express admonition of the Holy Ghost, but also by [Pg 138] the *overrulings of his Providence.* Take the account of the first dispersion. The Saviour ascended from the Mount of Olives, and the disciples returned to Jerusalem. The day of Pentecost arrived, and three thousand converts were added to their number. This multitude of believers was daily and rapidly increased. Here, then, was a very large city, the capital and pride of the nation, and a place of immense resort from all the nations round about. And in this city were many thousands of Christians, who were in peculiar need of constant care and faithful instruction, and had they been divided out to the pastoral care of the twelve apostles, would have made perhaps as large churches as any twelve in the city of New-York. Jerusalem then presented to the apostles a vast amount of pastoral care, and a field of labor unequalled perhaps in religious influence, considering the world as it then was, by any city that can be named within the limits of Christendom. The apostles were inclined to remain in Jerusalem, and considering the call for labor there, it is not wonderful that they were thus inclined. They seemed for a time to have forgotten the last command of their ascended Lord, and to have [Pg 139] chosen a work more resembling that of settled pastors. But the Saviour allowed a persecution to rage in the city, till first the great body of the church, and afterwards all the apostles, except James, were scattered abroad. So the great Jerusalem was left with but one apostle. Eleven of the twelve, who had become in a measure settled there, were driven abroad; and not from Jerusalem only, but without the limits of Palestine. Such is evidently the *fact.* Let every one draw from it the instruction it affords. To my mind it clashes irreconcilably with the present distribution of ministers.

Take another case. Paul had been laboring at Ephesus two whole years, and had collected a very large church in that city. This city was the emporium of Asia Minor; a place of much resort, and greatly celebrated throughout the known world. The large number of disciples there, who needed a pastor to warn them day and night with tears, and the wide door which was there opened for preaching the Gospel, presented such strong claims to the mind of Paul, as seemed likely to fix there his permanent abode. What pastor of the present day can urge stronger [Pg 140] reasons for continuing his charge, than Paul might have urged for continuing his relation to the large church at Ephesus? For in addition to a large city and a large church, the converts had been but lately gathered from heathenism—were but babes in Christ—and needed constant instruction and unwearied care. Yet God was pleased to allow Demetrius to excite an uproar, and thus to sever Paul from his church and congregation, and send him abroad into Macedonia. This is another *fact*—a stubborn fact, which we ought to bear in mind, and weigh well. If God saw best thus to break tender ties, separate Paul from a large city and a large body of such converts as, above all others, needed special care, and to leave the important post almost destitute, *can it be* his will that all the pastors of the present day should stay in their places, and that none of them should go forth to the heathen? If the city had been Boston, with its thousand means of grace, the case would have been comparatively weak; but it was Ephesus, a heathen city, and depending almost entirely on the living voice of Paul, and yet this one preacher must become a missionary. Let us look at this fact, and each [Pg 141] one for himself draw conclusions; not those that are wild and extravagant, but such as are *true and sober*.

We have here a commentary on the last command of Jesus. It was commented upon by the providence of God, separating the apostles from Jerusalem, Antioch, and Ephesus. It was commented upon by the direct admonition of the Holy Ghost in a particular case. It was commented upon by the practice of the apostles. Let us beware that we substitute not, for this correct commentary, any worldly-wise interpretation of our own. Let us admit it just as it comes to us from early days, fresh and unmodified, and allow it to govern our lives.

There are but few who do not admit, that the present distribution of ministers is anti-apostolic—that many, who are now pastors, ought to have become missionaries before they were settled. And can the mere fact of being settled have produced such a vast change in the question of duty, as to place it forever at rest? If the clustering together of twelve thousand ministers within the bounds of the United States, where a thousand means of grace and improvement exist besides the voice [Pg 142] of the living teacher, is a very different thing from going into all the world, and preaching the Gospel to every creature—an egregious disproportion to the wants of the world—must we stifle all emotion and all inquiry, in taking it for granted that it is now too late for change? And yet there seems to be a tacit understanding, that any other distribution than that now existing, of the *present generation* of ministers, is a point not to be agitated. At least, many a pastor quiets himself with the thought, that no change is to be contemplated in his particular case, for the care of a church is on his hands. Almost by common consent, pastors are excused; and missionaries are looked for from the young men and the children; and the hope of the heathen amounts to this, that some young men may be kept from imitating the example of their fathers and elder brethren, and be prevailed upon to enter the missionary work before they *become pastors*. For if the mere fact of being a pastor places the question at rest, young men will feel themselves relieved as soon as they enter that office.

I have known young men whose minds were goaded on the question of going to the [Pg 143] heathen, like the conscience of a convicted sinner, till a call was presented to some important church; and then they succeeded in laying the subject at once and entirely aside. Like the pursued ostrich, who thrusts her head into the sand, and vainly imagines that she is concealed from her pursuers, so, I fear, some endeavor to elude the convictions of conscience. I put the question to your own good sense, your candor, and your pious feelings: Can the mere fact of being a pastor excuse a man from going to the heathen, when perhaps he became a pastor in violation of the Saviour's command?

It is acknowledged, that many pastors ought to have become missionaries before they were settled—that the present amazing disproportion between settled ministers at home, and missionaries abroad, ought never to have existed. To argue so plain a case would be a waste of breath. How then can the fact of having wandered from duty excuse one from the performance of it? To-day, it is the duty of Jonah to go to Nineveh. To-morrow, he has engaged his passage to Tarshish, has paid his fare, has gone down into the sides of the ship, and is quietly at rest. Is he therefore [Pg 144] excused? To-day, the command of Christ presses upon me the obligation to go to the heathen. To-morrow, leaving out of mind this command, which still applies in all its force, I enter into an obligation with a particular church to take upon me its pastoral care: which obligation is binding? The last, do you say? Can I then thus easily thrust aside the Saviour's last and most impressive command? Can I, by such a course, shield myself effectually from its further application? I have yet to learn, that by any change of place or circumstances we can free ourselves from the weight of the Saviour's injunction. I mean not to assert, that all who ought to have become missionaries before they were settled, ought to become so now. Some have entirely hedged up their way; and though they may have been disobedient in doing so, yet deep regret and sincere repentance is all the reparation they can now make. But those who ought to have gone to the heathen, and before whom the door is still open for going, *such* should still become missionaries, and on the obvious principle, that it is better to do our duty late than not to do it all. The mere plea of being a pastor is not a sufficient ex [Pg 145] cuse; and it is losing too, continually, more and more of its force. It is a wonder that it should be relied upon so much as a *quietus*, since, in the present age, the residence of a pastor is very transient and uncertain.

Again let me say, it is a great thing, a good thing, and a rare thing, to be entirely honest in the sight of God. Let us endeavor to be so. It is to be feared, that there may be some who exempt themselves from becoming missionaries on the ground of being pastors, who are not altogether honest in their excuse. Are there not some individuals, who make it, who would manifest but little hesitation in leaving the pastoral office to take the oversight of a college, to become a professor in a theological seminary, or to take charge of some prominent religious periodical? When urged to become a missionary, the pastor pleads his attachment to his people; their affection for him, which gives him great influence; and his acquaintance with their prejudices, opinions, habits, and whole character, so as to adapt his instructions to their particular case. He mentions these, and the like considerations, and concludes very readily that he can be more useful in his present situation than in any [Pg 146] other. But when a presidency, a professorship, or a more influential church is offered, the reasons before urged seem to lose something of their force; and through the intervention of some new light, which I shall not account for, the conclusion is formed that another situation would be more *useful*. The motive for a change is a good one; but it is to be remembered that this same motive, that of being more useful, could not prevail upon them to become missionaries.

Facts of this kind could be collected, I think to a considerable extent; and they lead me, however unwilling, to suspect that, in some cases, the honest reason why ministers do not become missionaries is not that they are pastors, but something quite different.

Another fact, too, makes me suspicious that there is some lack of entire honesty. A pastor says he cannot become a missionary, for he has the care of a church. In a few months, for some cause or other, he is dismissed from his church and people. What does he do? become a missionary? I have one in my eye who was a pastor of a church in a large city. He told me, that nothing but his relation as pastor in that city could keep him a moment [Pg 147] from the missionary work. Soon after, he was dismissed from his church and people; and think you he became a missionary? You would betray a very limited knowledge of human nature to think so.

"But," says one, "I am opposed to fickleness and change." Ah! indeed; does it betray fickleness to leave a church to become a missionary? Did God favor fickleness and change when he prevented the permanent location of the apostles in Palestine, by a voice from heaven, and by violent persecutions? Did the Saviour favor fickleness in his last command? When a presidency, a professorship, or a more prominent and influential church is offered you, then speak of fickleness—the excuse may possibly be in place; but never, never in place, while untold millions of our race are dying for lack of vision, and our commission reads, "Go ye into all the world, and preach the Gospel to every creature."

One pastor excuses himself, by saying, "The attachment between me and my people is very dear, and this attachment gives me great influence with them." I reply, Was not [Pg 148] the attachment very dear between the apostles and the disciples at Jerusalem, and also between Paul and the converts at Antioch, and at Ephesus? What language of affection and solicitude can equal that of Paul for his converts? He calls them his "joy and crown"—the "little children for whom he travails in birth, till Christ be formed in them." He says to them, "I live, if ye stand fast in the Lord."

And had not the apostles great influence in the churches in which they labored? Had not Paul and Barnabas great influence in the church at Antioch? Did not the church love and respect them, and hang in breathless silence upon their lips, and look upon their departure as an irreparable loss? Yet, though entwined into the hearts of the people, and possessing every advantage to instruct them which intimate acquaintance and unbounded influence could give, the Holy Ghost, notwithstanding, said, "Separate me Barnabas and Saul."

Attachment is your plea; but the spirit of the Gospel is a spirit of self-denial, and requires us not only to forsake church and people, but also father and mother, brother and sister, son and daughter, and to hold our own lives [Pg 149] loosely. Those persons to whom attachment is strongest, and who *can't be spared* on that account, are the best fitted for missions.

You plead the *influence* which you possess with your church and people. This, instead of being a reason for remaining at home, is a powerful argument for going abroad. In that very influence you possess an advantage and qualification for the missionary work, which very few missionaries enjoy. It is greatly to be lamented that the church has but little acquaintance with her missionaries. It was not so in primitive times. On this account there is room for the question to arise, Whether there ought not to be less of the home minister for life, and the exile for life; a narrower gulf between the two, and more passing and repassing, as the apostles were wont to do; a breaking up of caste, grade and condition among ministers, as regards various fields—a more literal compliance with the precept of "going into all the world, and preaching the Gospel to every creature." Be this however as it may—for there is much that can be said on either side of the question—it is most certainly true, that the pastor possesses one very great advantage: that by going to the heathen [Pg 150] he can wake up, in one church at least, the spirit of doing good—the enterprising and benevolent spirit of Christ and his apostles. He may take with him, as helpers, some of its most intelligent and active members, and call forth the contributions and enlist the prayers of those who may remain.

It seems, that nothing less than such means as the separation of pastors for the work of missions, can avail to awake the slumbering churches, and to lead them to begin in earnest to seek the salvation of the heathen; to feel that the work presses upon them individually, and demands all their energies and their personal enlistment. For it is a sober and humiliating fact, as I have had some opportunity of judging, that there are few churches comparatively, in our land, who seem to have drunk deeply into the missionary spirit. There is need, therefore, of a movement on the part of pastors, to arouse the churches from their guilty slumbers.

A pastor possesses much influence with his church and congregation. The Lord then has given him five talents, and he can easily make them ten: by going abroad he can benefit his church perhaps as much as by remaining their [Pg 151] pastor, and, at the same time, be the instrument of saving many heathen souls. "There is that scattereth, and yet increaseth;" and "he that watereth shall be watered also himself." God's blessing distils upon the liberal soul, and the liberal church. The performance of duty is attended with the Saviour's smiles and a rich reward. Who does not see, that a pastor could in no way so effectually awaken in his church a spirit of benevolent feeling and action, as by exhibiting it in his own person; by rising up, and going forth to the heathen, urging a part of his flock to accompany him, and the rest to sustain him in the field? Who doubts, that by such a course he would do more to arouse the pure and active religion of Jesus Christ and his apostles, than he could possibly do in any other way; that he would give an impulse to his church in favor of primitive piety and practice, that should add vastly to its strength, its glory and its numbers, and be felt in all time to come. Let not the pastor, then, excuse himself from the missionary work, because he has acquired influence in his church and congregation; for that very fact is a powerful argument for going abroad. [Pg 152]

For the same reason, no one can excuse himself because he fills a *post of vast importance*. He is the pastor of an influential church, a president of a college, a professor in a theological seminary, the editor of a religious paper of immense circulation, or the secretary of some society: his station is one of vast responsibility, and he imagines that he is therefore excused from becoming a missionary. But was not Jerusalem an important place? more prominent, compared with other cities of that time, than any city in the United States? And yet all the apostles, except one, were required not only to leave that city, but to go without the limits of Palestine. Was not Antioch as important as Boston or Philadelphia? Yet Paul and Barnabas were not suffered to remain there.

Besides, is not the work of a missionary a difficult, important, and responsible work? The Holy Spirit thought so in apostolic times. When a man was needed to preach to Cornelius and his household, a man of no less ability and influence than Peter was chosen. When a man was called to go to Antioch, Barnabas was sent, a man of great piety and influence. And when two of the five preach [Pg 153] ers at Antioch were called to go to the heathen, the Holy Ghost did not choose Simeon, or Lucius, or Manaen, but said, "Separate me Barnabas and Saul;" the men of the greatest ability, experience, piety and wisdom. Thus the Holy Spirit seemed to declare that the work of a missionary required greater talents, more mature wisdom, and deeper piety, than the work of a pastor in the largest and most influential churches.

And is not this doctrine, while it accords with the instructions of the Holy Ghost and the practice of primitive times, also a dictate of common sense? Would you choose weak men to penetrate into the very midst of the enemy, and to grapple with the Anaks of the land, and keep those who are strong in a garrison at home? Would you select indifferent statesmen to settle the affairs of revolutionary France, or to reduce to order the chaotic mass of the South American states; and employ the able, the wise and talented, in governing a country already quiet and peaceful? Did it require less wisdom to lay the foundation and form the constitution of our good government, than it requires to manage the state on principles already established? [Pg 154] Does it require less skill to draft the plan of a capitol, than to work at the building when the plan is mature? Does it require less wisdom to govern a camp in a state of mutiny, than when in subjection and at peace? Look, then, at the work of missions. Does it require less talent to deal with minds clouded by ignorance, perverted by superstition, and barred by arrogance, bigotry, and pride, than to instruct the unbiassed, the willing, and intelligent? Does it require less wisdom to tear up the foundations of heathen society, and lay it anew on the principles of the Gospel — to change society morally, religiously, and socially, than to preserve in a good condition a people already intelligent, industrious, and Christian? Surely, if talent is needed anywhere in the kingdom of Christ, it is in the missionary work. That minister, whose talents and piety make him so useful at home that he *cannot be spared*, that is the minister who is needed abroad. The foreign field calls for no laborers who can be conveniently spared.

Then, is the church of a pastor wealthy and influential? It is the very church that needs to be aroused by his leaving it. Or is he connected with a literary, or theological [Pg 155] institution? Some thus connected are needed to go, to produce the best impression on the young men who are in training. The more important and influential then one's place is, the more like a rushing flood do reasons crowd upon him to arise and go.

It is very common for men to excuse themselves from the work of missions, on the ground, that they are somewhat *advanced in years*. There is weight in this excuse. That person would exhibit the want of a proper balance of mind, who should urge all indiscriminately, whatever their age and however circumstanced in life, to go forth to the heathen. But still the excuse of age ought to be looked at cautiously.

Age implies experience, authority, dignity, and wisdom — the very qualities most wanted in the difficult work of missions. The work of tearing up and laying anew the foundations of society, moral, religious, and social, is a task that ought by no means to be committed to the young and inexperienced. It is preposterous to commit altogether to novices in the ministry a work so new, so complicated, so beset with difficulties, on the right hand and on the left, and so momentous, too, in [Pg 156] its responsibilities. Can Satan be driven so easily from his own territory, that none but raw troops are needed for the contest? Can the broad and deep intrenchments of Paganism, Mohammedism, and Romanism be so easily taken, as not to need men of age, experience and skill, to direct the assault? Can the snares in which the heathen are held; which are laid with all the subtlety of the arch-fiend, be so easily divested of their specious character, and traced into their thousand windings, as not to require the wisdom and experience of age? A minister has age: he has then one great qualification for the work. "Paul the aged" had none too much experience, dignity and wisdom, for the work of a missionary to heathen lands.

But age, it is said, is a great barrier in acquiring a foreign language. There is force in this remark; but let us be cautious, that we do not trust too much to it. A great amount of labor may be performed on heathen ground without a knowledge of the language. Much can be done in the English language, and much, too, can be done through interpreters. All that David Brainerd accomplished was in this way. [Pg 157]

But how certain is it, that persons somewhat advanced cannot acquire a foreign language? This plea is not peculiar to those who have been some time in the ministry. No excuse is more frequently offered, and with more appearance of honesty, even in the college and the theological seminary. It is difficult to place the mark of age where this excuse may be properly offered, and where it may not. Shall we place it at thirty-five? Some missionaries now in the field entered on the work at that age, and acquired the language without much difficulty. It may be remarked, too, that men of traffic abroad, from youth to gray hairs, usually learn so much of a foreign language as to answer their purpose. Let us beware, then, *how much* we depend on the excuse of age; and be cautious, too, *how far up* the scale of years we place the mark.

Another excuse which has some weight is this: "I must remain at home *to take care of my aged parents.*" So said one to Christ: "Lord, I will follow thee, but suffer me first to go and bury my father." Jesus answered, "Let the dead bury their dead, but go thou and preach the Gospel." I leave to the reader [Pg 158] to determine the precise meaning and force of this reply of our Saviour. This much it certainly means, that some *may* excuse themselves from preaching to take care of their parents, when the excuse is not valid. I will not say, that the excuse is not sufficient in some cases; but I am inclined to think that such cases are rare. A parent must be *very* dependent upon a son, to be liable to such inconvenience and suffering from his absence, as can reasonably weigh in the balance against the claims of the hundreds of millions of dying heathen.

But the excuse which seems to be the most valid, is this: "My going to the heathen is out of the question, for *I have a family of children*." This is indeed a tender point. God has given me some experience on this subject, and I know how to appreciate the excuse. But the Saviour says, "He that loveth son or daughter more than me, is not worthy of me." This declaration means nothing, unless it requires us to make great sacrifices in regard to our children. So far as we can at present see, the world cannot be converted without great self-denial on this point. Precisely what sacrifices are to be made in [Pg 159] regard to children, is a question which is not, as yet, fully determined.

But let us look at the excuse. If a minister may *stay* at home because he has children, may not the missionary who has children *return* home? A pastor has one child, and cannot go. Then may not the missionary who has one child, come back? A pastor has six children, and cannot go. Many missionaries have six children, shall not they return? The mere circumstance of being already abroad cannot have much weight; and the sacrifice of a voyage in such a question, and among a multitude of other weighty reasons, is scarcely worth being named. If children then are an excuse, let missionaries return. No, you say; missionaries who have children must not return on that account. What then shall they do with their children? Keep them, and train them up to be helpers in the work? Let pastors then take their children into the field, and train them up for that purpose. You certainly have hearts too noble to impose a burden on the shoulders of others which you would not bear yourselves. Your children would have the advantage of the children of missionaries, having been thus far [Pg 160] trained in a Christian land. As to future advantages of education, they will have the same with the children now abroad. You certainly cannot complain of equality.

But, you say, let missionaries send their children home. Then let pastors leave their children at home and go abroad. Ah, you say, pastors cannot endure the thought; it would be a shock to their parental feelings that they cannot sustain. But, I ask, have missionaries no feelings? have their hearts become hard, like blocks of wood and pieces of rock? Does love to Christ, and compassion for the heathen, tend to make men and women obtuse in their feelings, so that a father or mother on heathen ground does not feel as intensely for the present and eternal welfare of a child, as a parent who has never gone to the heathen? Ah! had you seen what my eyes have witnessed, facts then should speak and I would be silent. Missionaries, indeed, are trained to cast their care upon God; their feelings are chastened and disciplined, but at the same time deep and intense. To a thousand dangers, toils and hardships, they may be inured; but when the separation of children is thought of, they show [Pg 161] full well that they are no proof against an agony of feeling. Certainly, then, you will not plead for exemption. You would not place upon others this burden, and pull away your own shoulders from it. You have souls too generous and benevolent to do that. You cannot find it in your hearts to offer to the lips of others a cup more bitter than you would drink yourselves. You can choose guardians for your children far better than the missionaries can who are abroad, and your children shall have the same provision for their support and education as theirs have.

We have glanced at some excuses. Many others there are in this excuse-making age. Be entreated to look at them with the command of Christ, a sinking world and a coming judgment, in your eye, and as far as they have weight and *no farther* be influenced by them. Where exemption cannot honestly be pleaded, the command in all its force is binding.

That some pastors of influence and talent should become missionaries, seems necessary; for *how otherwise can the means be raised to sustain missions abroad, and to send forth young men who may offer themselves*? It is well known, that operations abroad have been [Pg 162] and are still exceedingly crippled. It is well known, too, that quite a company of young men have at different times been waiting, for want of requisite funds to send them forth to the heathen.

Now this is the state of things, not because there is not money enough in the hands of Christians—no one imagines that such is the fact—but because Christians, as a body, are not aroused to duty. What means shall be taken to arouse them? I, for one, am inclined to think that there would be hope, if some influential and prominent pastors would enter the missionary work. In such a case, I should indeed have strong hope that the impulse, falling in with the spirit of primitive practice and the will of the Holy Ghost, would be such as to bring forth the funds needed to sustain the operations now begun, send forth waiting young men, and carry themselves also into the field. I feel quite confident, that the measure would soon clear the seaboard of all who might be detained, and place their joyful feet on foreign soil.

The great body of professed Christians are becoming luxurious in their modes of life. One cannot go through the churches, after the [Pg 163] absence of several years, without being forcibly impressed with this fact. They press forward after wealth, and profess to be accumulating it for Christ; but in the end, spend it on themselves and on their children. Now what, under God, shall break up this covetousness, and luxurious manner of life? What shall bring them back to the pure and unadulterated principles of the Gospel—to live, labor, and die for Christ, as did the primitive disciples? Let pastors, like the apostles, go into all the world and preach the Gospel to every creature. There is reason to hope that the church members would likewise imbibe the right spirit, and act on right principles. Then we should hear no more of schools disbanded and missionaries detained, but troops of heralds would be carrying out the news of salvation and sending back tidings of success. There is much philosophical and Bible truth in the proverb, "Like people like priest." O, what responsibility rests on the ministers of Christ!

Again, if all settled ministers of talent and influence remain at home, how can such a number of missionaries be secured as seem needed for the world's conversion? If many [Pg 164] of those already in the sacred office do not go, it is absolutely certain, that the present generation of heathen must die without the Gospel. The angel of death continues hovering over the dying nations, mowing down his twenty millions a year; and before ministers can be raised up from among the youth and children, will be drawing a stroke at the last man of all that are now heathen. The present generation of ministers must preach the Gospel to the present generation of mankind. It will be the duty of the next generation of ministers to preach to the inhabitants that shall be then on the globe. To look for missionaries from among the young alone, is making no provision for the present generation of heathen. If the heathen are to be left till missionaries can be trained up, they are to be left—the soul shudders at the thought—till they shall be in hell! By making this postponement, the churches, in effect, though certainly without intending it, sign the death warrant of a great portion of the present six hundred millions of perishing heathen; relinquish all effort for this vast multitude, and only dream of saving the next generation—of whom it would be a mercy never to be born, [Pg 165] unless there shall be more hope of their salvation than can be seen at present—*dream*, I say, of saving the next generation; for to think much of raising up the young to be missionaries, without going ourselves, is little better than dreaming.

To induce young men, to any great extent, to become missionaries, when their fathers and elder brethren do not, is hopeless. Precept must become more powerful than example, before such a result can take place. How can you so blindfold the young, stop their ears, and wall them off from surrounding influences, as to expect such a result? If their eyes are left open, what do they see? They see their fathers and elder brethren settled at home, and some of them in quiet, comfort and honor. If their ears are left open, what do they hear? They hear various excuses for remaining at home, and among others, the specious idea of training up children to be missionaries. And what will they do? They will dream of training your grandchildren for missions, and your grandchildren dream of training the next generation, and so on, as the sixty generations past have done, from the time of the Saviour down. But the fire of God's Spirit shall burn [Pg 166] up this chaff. The world shall not be cheated out of its millenium. The judgment trumpet shall not sound before the arrival of the latter day glory.

To become a missionary, in the present state of things, is sailing against wind and tide; so that those who find their way to the heathen, compared with the number who ought to go, are very few indeed. To urge a large number into the field is hopeless. Bonaparte might as well have urged his soldiers over the Alps without leading them. We cannot expect the nature of things to change, and precept to become more powerful than example. A portion of the more talented of the settled ministry must lead the way. Then there shall be found a resuscitating principle; our eyes shall beam with joy, and we shall fondly cherish a rational hope of the world's renovation.

Again, many pastors should become missionaries, for all things await their personal enlistment in the service. God, in his providence, is causing a state of preparation in the world which calls for some mighty movement on the part of the church. A door is opened into almost every nation on the earth, and [Pg 167] ships are ready to carry us to almost every port. Now is the time for a great effort. All the elements are ready for action, and need only to be brought to bear on the glorious cause of the world's conversion. To effect this, there must be a high stand of prayerful enterprise on the part of the present generation of ministers. The Lord has brought us to the ministry for such a time as this; and surely my brethren will not prove themselves unworthy of so vast a responsibility, but come up joyfully to the work, and reap the harvest of the world.

And here let me say, that the millions of souls already lost are immense; and it would be awfully presumptuous in Christians to neglect the millions and hundreds of millions of the present generation. Century after century has rolled along, ingulfing generation after generation, till one would think that Satan himself would be satisfied with the enormous havoc. Eighteen centuries have passed away, and sixty generations, five hundred millions each—thirty billions of immortal souls left to perish since Christ gave command to evangelize them. Are not thirty billions enough? Shall we, by any guilty neglect, suffer the [Pg 168] present generation, six hundred millions more, to be added? O, let the billions of souls already lost suffice. O, let us arise, and go and preach the Gospel to the nations, that the generations that remain between this and the judgment may be saved.

Let me suggest, too, that nothing would so readily produce *union among ministers at home*, as to divert all their powers of body and mind into some all-absorbing and self-denying enterprise. Now, what angel of heaven has not wept over the contentions and jealousies that cloud the glory of the American churches. How has the heart of Jesus bled over the dissensions and strife of his own ministers! And is there no remedy? Let pastors become so engrossed in fulfilling their commission as to obey its literal import, and arise and go; and I mistake much, if the movement would not make a material impression on their contentions and jealousies. They would feel that they were doing a great work, and could not come down.

For contention they would find neither time nor inclination. It would be difficult to state, in a foreign tongue, their metaphysical distinctions, so as to make a difference. Higher and nobler objects [Pg 169] would engross the soul. Be entreated to try this course. Then the recording angel shall not be compelled, with aching heart and streaming eyes, to inscribe "Ichabod" on our American Zion; but, with willing soul and ready hands, shall write in fairer lines, "Beautiful for situation, the joy of the whole earth."

But it is often said, "I never *felt* it to be my duty to go to the heathen: I never had any such impression."

No such impression! Did then the command of our ascended Lord, his *last* command, delivered under the most solemn circumstances, make no impression upon you? Did the temporal and eternal miseries of six hundred millions of your fellow men make no impression upon you? Did their groans and sighs, which came over the waters like the voice of seven thunders, peal after peal, make no impression upon you? And could you remain at home with comfort and peace of mind, with the weeping and wailing of millions of dying souls in your ears, backed up with the command of Christ to go and seek their salvation? While Jesus plead, "Lo, I died for them, go, preach my Gospel [Pg 170] to them, that they may live;" could you remain unimpressed and unmoved? And have all these considerations, and a hundred more, been urged upon you for years, and yet failed to make an *impression*? Alas! of what is your heart made, that it does not feel? Look for no *supernatural* impression. Missionaries have none. There is no need of any. He that can live and not be impressed, may well tremble for his own salvation. It appears that you are easily impressed that it is your duty to remain at home. The motives, I fear, that come before your mind are well suited to make an impression. You quickly perceive a *call*, when country, home, friends, the endearments of society, and the like considerations crowd upon your mind. O, dear brethren, let us be *entirely honest*, as we expect soon to meet the Saviour and the world of perishing souls for whom he died.

Another similar excuse is often made: "Did I possess the requisite attainments in holiness, I should delight to go abroad. But as the case is, I cannot become a missionary: I have not piety enough."

Not piety enough! Then be entreated to become more pious without delay. As you [Pg 171] value the souls of dying men, defer not to become more holy. Through your want of piety the heathen may be left to perish. But what is holiness? Is it not obedience to the commands of Christ? Obey, then, his last command: *that will be becoming more holy.* Go forth to the heathen from love to Christ: that will be becoming more pious. "Not piety enough!" Will you presume to offer that excuse to the Lord Jesus, when you shall stand before him to render account for the blood of the heathen? And when you shall see multitudes of the heathen sinking into hell, whom, under the blessing of the Spirit, you might have saved; and hear their weeping, wailing, and gnashing of teeth; will it ease your mind, and quiet your conscience, that you had not piety enough to go and make known to them the way of life? This is a solemn subject. Let us try, dear brethren, to look at it as we ought.

Allied to this excuse is the following: "I have never thought myself qualified for the work of missions. It is a work which in my view requires rare endowments. Did I possess the requisite qualifications, I should delight to engage in so glorious a work." [Pg 172]

To this excuse I would say, There is room in the wide field of missions for every grade and variety of talent. Such is the universal testimony of those who have gone forth. Neither could it be otherwise in so various and vast a work as that of converting all nations, many of whom need to be instructed in the simplest arts of civilized life, and in the very alphabet of knowledge. But the excuse you render is entirely at variance with the facts in the case. If the work of missions be deemed worthy of the greatest talents, why is it that a large number do not go forth from among the more prominent and influential in the sacred office? The plea of disqualification is a popular one. There is in it much appearance of humility and self-depreciation. But facts testify, that many who plead their want of talent do not hesitate, if invited, to take upon them the care of a college, or of a large and opulent church. If the conduct of men is to be regarded as a just interpreter of their sentiments, then the great body of the Christian ministry, instead of regarding themselves unfit for the work of missions, consider themselves too well qualified to enter it. They really think, that those of inferior qualifica [Pg

173] tions will do for missions; while those of superior minds and brilliant talents must be reserved for important stations at home.

It is said again, "*All* cannot go abroad."

I reply, Do not use the word "all" till there shall be some need of it. There is no danger *yet* that the home company will be comparatively too small.

There is another excuse which is worthy of more notice. One says, "My own country claims my first attention. It presents a field of vast extent, and demands a vast amount of labor. Its schools, colleges and seminaries, must be sustained. Its religious periodicals must be edited. The churches must be watched over, and brought up to a higher standard of piety. Revivals must be promoted. But passing by these claims for labor, look at the wide-spreading desolations of the West, where ignorance, infidelity, and Romanism prevail, and threaten, at no very future day, to be the overthrow of our government — the extinguishment of our dearly-bought and precious inheritance. All our exertions must be put forth to save our country; for the progress of light and knowledge throughout the world depends on its existence. [Pg 174] The overthrow of our government would put back the dial of the moral world ten centuries. Our own nation lost, and what would become of the heathen? when would the millenium arrive? Our present attention must be directed to the salvation of our own country, and our missionary exertions must be concentrated on the West."

The excuse does not stop here; but a citizen from Great Britain would say, "I too must speak in behalf of my country — a country whose possessions encircle the globe. The existence and religious prosperity of a nation whose commerce is so great, and whose dominions embrace a large portion of the heathen world, cannot but be intimately connected with the universal prevalence of light and peace. It is of the first importance, that the *heart* of such a nation should beat with a healthy pulse; that much effort should be made to promote a high standard of vital godliness in the universities and churches at home. But more than this, look at the vast body of laboring men in England and Ireland, who are living in ignorance and in sin. They call loudly for teachers and for preachers of the Gospel, and ought to receive, for the pres [Pg 175] ent at least, all we can educate and all we can support."

In reply to this excuse I would first say, Let us look a moment at the conclusion to which we are reduced. "The United States cannot furnish missionaries, for the present at least; far less can Great Britain; and still less the Continent of Europe." The inevitable conclusion is, that the present generation of heathen must be left to perish. Six hundred millions of our race must be deliberately relinquished to endure the agonies of eternal death. But what is the plea that so readily leaves the millions of ignorant heathen to hopelessness and despair? "We must go to the West." "We must direct our efforts to the laboring class of England and Ireland." Then, I say, be consistent, and actually *do* what you profess. As yet, how many of the learned, the eloquent and influential of the ministry, have become missionaries at the West? Some have gone to the West, to be presidents of colleges there; but how many have gone to engage in the more appropriate duties of the *missionary*? And in Great Britain, how many have left their professorships in the universities, and their wealthy churches, [Pg 176] to labor as *missionaries* among the ignorant class of society in England and Ireland? O! the West, and the ignorant class in England and Ireland, would lift up their hearts to God in gratitude if you would go forth to the heathen: for the reflex influence of such a course would scatter among them the means of grace as thick as the stars of heaven, and as bright as the sun in his glory. I could almost assert, from personal observation, that every missionary to the heathen sends ten to the West. If men are pressed to go to China, they cannot stop short of the West. Besides, have you forgotten the nature of benevolence? If you wish to strengthen it, to increase it and expand it, so as to be the means of saving the United States, and of saving Great Britain, then bring it into exercise. Let the church impart liberally of what she has, both of men and money. She will have the more left, paradoxical as the assertion may at first seem. Let the principle of benevolence be aroused in the churches, and it is literally inexhaustible in its resources, both of money and of men; for the more it exhausts the more it still possesses. This is not mere missionary philosophy, but Bible doctrine; and so plainly [Pg 177] inculcated, that he that doubts it is a novice in the Scriptures, and a babe in the school of

Christ. There is a backwardness, an apathy and deadness in the ministry, and in the churches; and it is therefore that infidelity and Romanism prevail at the West, and that the ignorant class in England and Ireland remain in wretchedness. The great thing needed is that the spirit of benevolence, the spirit of Christ, or in other words true religion, be aroused in the churches. And in no way can you so effectually do it as by giving yourself to the missionary work. God's wisdom is very much at variance with the cold, calculating, short-sighted and sin-blinded wisdom of man. Let us follow heavenly wisdom, as laid down in the Bible: "Give," "Go," and thereby save ourselves, our country, and the world. *That nation that obeys God* shall prosper. Let us try the Bible philosophy of saving the United States and Great Britain, by obeying God—by going forth and teaching all nations.

[Pg 178]

CHAPTER VII.

IMPORT OF THE GREAT COMMISSION.

The Founder of the church was a missionary. The church is a *missionary band*, professedly aiming to carry out the design of its Founder, in the wide field of the World. The commission to the apostles is the commission to Christ's ministers in every age. This commission, it is to be feared, is losing much of its force from misinterpretation.

That a construction somewhat incorrect is placed by some ministers on the commission which they hold, seems to be evident; for how otherwise should an impression obtain, that there is something *peculiar* about the office of the missionary—that his commission is quite different from that of other ministers of Christ.

Let the commission of both the minister at home and missionary abroad be exhibited and read. The terms, word for word, are the same. It is unhappy, extremely so, that a *peculiarity* is thrown about the word *missionary*, [Pg 179] since the New Testament authorizes no such distinction. Both ministers at home and those abroad claim to be successors of the apostles or first missionaries, whose letter of instructions, short but explicit, reads thus: "Go ye into all the world, and preach the Gospel to every creature." This is the commission of every ambassador, and no one, at home or abroad, can consistently hold his office any longer than he continues to act in accordance with its import.

The Saviour is all-wise, and knew precisely what commission to give. He carefully chose every word in which it is expressed. The apostles showed by their conduct how they understood it—that they knew what was meant by "all the world" and "every creature." Now, I ask, how can such a construction be placed on these obvious phrases, as to make it consistent for about eleven thousand eight hundred ministers out of twelve thousand to stay in the United States, and about the same proportion in Great Britain? The apostles showed by their conduct what they understood by the word "Go." By what reasoning, I ask, has it been made to mean, in fifty-nine cases out of sixty, *send, contribute*, [Pg 180] *and educate young men*? If an inhabitant of another planet should visit this earth, and see ministers clustered together in a few favored spots, could you make him believe that they hold in their hands the commission first delivered to the apostles?

Would it be thought dutiful, in military officers, to treat the orders of their commander-in-chief as we do the command of our Master; or in mercantile agents, to interpret thus loosely the instructions of their employers? The perversion, however, has become so familiar to us, that we are insensible of it; and the fact may be numbered among other wonders of a like kind, which the experience of a few past years has exhibited. A few years since, good men were in the use of intoxicating drinks without dreaming it a sin; and so now we may be shaping our course very wide from the command of our Saviour, and yet think not of the guilt we incur.

The misconstruction has become so universal, and so firmly established — the true and obvious interpretation buried so deep in the
rubbish of things gone by — that all books written on ministerial
duty, which I have seen, take it for granted that the persons [Pg 181]
addressed, for the most part at least, are to preach and labor among
a people who have long had the Gospel. And may I not inquire —
and I would do it with due deference and respect — Do not lectures
on pastoral theology in the schools of the prophets take it too much
for granted, that the hearers are to labor in Christian lands? Is not
the business of going into all the world, and preaching the Gospel to
every creature, regarded, practically at least, as an *exception*, for
which there need be no provision in books or lectures? If Paul were
to write or lecture on pastoral theology, would he not give more
prominence to the duties that might devolve upon his students in
foreign lands? Would he not, indeed, make the work of missions
stand forth as *the* work, and not as an exception or a peculiarity?

Few men, in these last days, can quiet their consciences, and yet
live in entire neglect of the heathen. Almost all professed Christians
feel that they must have some interest in the great enterprise. To
begin to act just as the last command of Christ requires, in its plain
literal import, as the apostles understood it, would be a hard and
self-denying service. What then shall they do? Will they operate [Pg
182] *by proxy*? This is the charming suggestion, by which often conscience is lulled to sleep and the heathen are left to perish.

It is true that many, and perhaps most, must aid in the work by
proxy — by training up others, by sending them forth, by encourag-
ing them, and by furnishing the necessary means. But the error is,
that all, with the exception of perhaps one minister out of sixty, and
one layman out of three thousand, are inclined so to act. It is wonderful with what electrical rapidity the soothing suggestion has
spread abroad. It is so insidious and speciously good, that it has
found its way, like an angel of light, to the best hearts and holiest
places. Indeed, it is a point very difficult to be determined; and
many judge no doubt with perfect correctness, when they decide to
act in this way. The danger consists in the eager rush and universal
resort. To be sensible that there is such a rush, begin and enumerate.
Directors and officers of various societies — and they are not few — of
theological seminaries too, and of colleges, think they are employed

in furnishing the requisite men, the requisite means, and the requisite instrumentalities, and so are preaching to the [Pg 183] heathen by proxy. Among ministers, the talented and eloquent, the learned and the influential, think they must labor in the important field at home; keep the churches in a state to operate upon the world, and so preach to the heathen by proxy. Ministers generally, about eleven thousand eight hundred out of twelve thousand, are zealous for training up young men, and think in that way of preaching to the heathen by proxy. Pious men of wealth, and those who are in circumstances to acquire wealth, or imagine that they have a talent to acquire it, profess to be accumulating the necessary means, and to be thus preaching to the heathen by proxy. Sabbath-school teachers, fathers and mothers, are fond of the notion of raising up children to be missionaries, and of thus preaching by proxy. Proxy is the universal resort. Now *some* proxy effort, and much indeed, is proper and indispensable; but must it not strike every mind, that such a universal and indiscriminate resort to it is utterly unreasonable?

How often do we hear the exhortation, "Let mothers consecrate their children to the missionary work in their earliest infancy. Let them be taught, as they grow up, that to [Pg 184] labor among the heathen is the most glorious work on earth. Let teachers in Sabbath-schools impart such instructions, and ministers in their pulpits. Let ministers and elders search out young men, urge them to engage in the work of missions, and let the churches educate them for that end, and pray for them that their zeal fail not. Let no pains be spared and no efforts be wanting, to raise up and send forth a large body of young men to labor for the heathen."

Now in regard to such an effort, every reflecting mind can see that it must be insufficient, if not hopeless. To succeed thus, as I have already said, precept must become more powerful than example. Commit the work of converting the world to your children, and they will commit it to your grandchildren. Try instruction in the nursery, try instruction in the Sabbath-school, try instruction from the pulpit: it will fall powerless as a ray of moonlight on a lake of ice, while contradicted by the *example* of mothers, of Sabbath-school teachers, and of ministers. Urge young men into the missionary field without going yourselves? A general might as well urge his army over the Alps without [Pg 185] leading them. Consecrate them to the work? Would it not be an unholy consecration—a consecration at the hands of those who were not themselves consecrated? The command does not say, *send*, but "Go." Let us then go, and urge others to *come*. We shall find this mode of persuasion the most effectual.

Let us commit to proxy that work which is pleasant and easy, and betake ourselves in person to those kinds of labor that are more self-denying, and to those posts that are likely to be deserted. This is the only principle of action that will secure success in any enterprise within the range of human efforts. Suppose the opposite principle is acted upon—that every one seeks for himself the most easy and pleasant work, and the most delightful and honorable station, and leaves for others the most obscure, the most self-denying, and the most perilous. Discover such a spirit in any enterprise, secular or religious, and it requires not the gift of prophecy to predict a failure. Practical and business men understand full well the truth and force of this remark. The true method is this: if there is a work that is likely to be neglected on account of its obscurity or self-denial, let every one, first of all, [Pg 186] see that *that* service is attended to. And if there is a post likely to be left deserted on account of its hardships or its perils, let every one be sure, first of all, that *that* post is occupied. Let there be an emulation among all to do the drudgery of the service, and to man the Thermopylæ of danger. Then you shall read in the vigor and nerve of the action the certainty of success.

In this way Bonaparte conquered Europe. If a portion of his army was likely to fall back, there the general pressed forward in person, inspiring courage and firmness. If all others shrunk from the deadly breach, thither he rushed, at once, with the flower of his army.

This principle of action is not more indispensable in the conquests of war, than in the great enterprise of the world's conversion. And how truly glorious, how sublime by contrast, to exhibit this principle of action, not in destroying mankind, but in laboring for their salvation! Let all Christians be filled with this spirit, let every redeemed sinner adopt in practice this rule of action, *to do the most self-denying, the most difficult and perilous work in person, and to commit the easiest to proxy*, then there would be a sight of moral sublim [Pg

187] ity that earth has not seen—all the elements in action that are needed, under God, to usher in the millenial day.

O, if to angels were committed the instrumentality of the world's conversion, where would Gabriel speed his way if not to the post of peril, and to the post of self-denying and toilsome drudgery? I mistake his character much, if he would not betake himself at once to the most arduous service. O, how he would delight to come down and labor with the lowest being on New Holland or New Guinea, and be the instrument of raising him up to the throne of Jesus! But to angels is not committed the stewardship of propagating that precious Gospel, which God has ordained for the world's renovation. The infinite treasure is placed in our hands, the immense responsibility is thrown upon us. O, let us prove ourselves worthy of such a trust, and not become traitorous to the cause, by falling into the general spirit of operating by proxy.

But, in truth, how far do we act on the principle named, that of performing in person the most arduous service, and of leaving the most pleasant work for others? Look over [Pg 188] the desolate and secluded parts of the United States; look over the heathen world, and make out an answer. Let facts speak. Is a residence in Arkansas preferred to a residence in New-York, or a voyage to New Guinea before one to Europe?

Our blessed Saviour and his apostles did not feel inclined to shrink from the more self-denying service, and to shift it upon others. If they had felt so, then we should have continued in a state of darkness, and have known full well the import of present wretchedness and eternal woe.

Let us suppose, for a moment, that the apostles had made the discovery of obeying by proxy the Saviour's last command. But I hesitate to make such a supposition, lest the force of such an immense contrast should make it to be regarded as a caricature upon the operations of the present age. In other words, our efforts to convert the world become so clumsy, slow and inefficient, from a lack of the right spirit and enough of it, in ministers and in the churches, that to impute the same kind and degree of effort to the apostles and primitive Christians, might excite a smile, rather than a sigh; and be deemed an attempt [Pg 189] to ridicule what is at present done, rather than an earnest, serious, and solemn expostulation. Such a result I should deplore. But if my readers will believe me to be aiming simply, with weeping eyes and an aching heart, to illustrate with force my own defects and their short-comings in duty, by detecting and tracing out a wrong principle of action, I will venture cautiously to make the supposition.

The words of the last command have fallen from the lips of the ascended Saviour, and the apostles assemble to deliberate how they shall carry them into execution. In the first place, Peter delivers an address. It is an able and thrilling discourse. He seems impatient to wing his way to foreign lands. After the discourse, they form themselves into a society. Arrangements being made, and the machinery being complete, they send forth John to solicit funds. He finds the disciples willing to contribute on an average, after much urging, about twenty-four cents each. A pittance of money is obtained, and then they search for a man. They thought Peter would be ready to go, from the speech he delivered, but he wishes to be excused: he has a family to support. They then fall upon various plans: some [Pg 190] think of training up young men to go forth, and others exhort parents to infuse a missionary spirit into their children. At length, however, it is found that one of the twelve begins to feel that he has a call to go—but this would be at the rate of one thousand from the twelve thousand ministers in the United States. This one man is sent forth to "go into all the world, and to preach the Gospel to every creature." The rest of the apostles sustain the various offices of the society, and have charge of important posts in Jerusalem, and in the cities and villages round about. They meet yearly, to deliberate upon the missionary enterprise. Some feel much, and humbly pray, and some say eloquent things about the glorious cause, and tell how they have found a fulcrum, where to place the lever of Archimides to elevate the world.

Now I ask most solemnly, and in a spirit of grief and humiliation, how such a course of conduct would have appeared in the apostles? Would it have evinced a spirit of obedience? Believe me, in early times, a readiness to obey supplied a great deal of machinery. Bring back into the ministers of the present day the spirit of the apostles, and into the churches [Pg 191] the spirit of the early disciples, and operations at once would be more simple and more efficient. A backwardness in duty—a disposition, if we do anything for the heathen, to do it by proxy, *this* is it that makes the wheels so ponderous and encumbered. "The letter killeth, but the Spirit giveth life." Give us the spirit, and annihilate the notion of operating so much by proxy, and we shall soon see a multitude of angels flying in the midst of heaven, having the everlasting Gospel to preach to the nations.

There is *no cheap or easy way of converting the world.* It is to be feared that some fall into the contrary notion, because they do not wish to believe that *all* they possess is needed in the work of the Lord, and that there is absolute necessity that they themselves go to the heathen. It is to be feared, that it is for this reason that so many are ready to imagine that the work is to be done by a few men, and a small amount of means. It would seem they expect to form lines of these few men, and encircle the globe in various directions; to place them on prominent points, like light-houses, and leave each with his single lamp to dispel the darkness of [Pg 192] a wide circumference. They seem to imagine that nations can be elevated from a degradation many ages deep, and thoroughly transformed, religiously, morally, mentally and socially, by the influence of a few missionaries, scattered here and there on some high eminences of the earth: that a single missionary, under a withering atmosphere, is to be preacher, physician, teacher, lawyer, mechanic, and everything that is necessary in raising a whole community from the inconceivable degradation of heathenism, up to the elevation of an industrious, intelligent, and Christian people.

Neither are the expectations formed by many, of mission seminaries, less visionary. A school, with two or three teachers, limited accommodations and small funds, with all its school-books to make, and the whole literature to form, is expected to accomplish all the work of the academy, college, and theological seminary, and speedily to transform untutored savages into able preachers of the Gospel.

And it is expected, by not a few, of the wife of the missionary—though living under a burning sun, in a house of poor accommodations, with unfaithful domestics, or none at [Pg 193] all; that notwithstanding, she will not only attend to the arduous duties of the household and educate her own children, but teach a school among the people, and superintend the female portion of the congregation—a task which a minister's wife in a Christian land, and under a bracing air, does not often attempt.

Now, would it be really a benefit to the church thus to flatter her indolence and her avarice, and convert the heathen with a fraction of wealth and a handful of men? Be assured, God loves the church too well thus to pamper a luxurious and self-indulgent spirit: he will allow no cheap and easy way of accomplishing the work. The object is worth more: worthy not only of the combined wealth of Christendom, but worthy also of the energies, the toil, and the blood if necessary, of the greatest and holiest men. It will not be in consistence with God's usual providence that a victory so noble should be achieved, till the treasures of the church shall be literally emptied in the contest, and the precious blood of thousands and tens of thousands of her ablest and best men poured out on the field. The work has already cost the [Pg 194] blood of God's only Son; and the prosecution and finishing of it shall be through toil, self-denial, entire devotement, and obedience even unto death.

Some rules that may be of use in agitating the question of becoming missionaries.

1. Guard against an *excuse-making* spirit. This is an age of excuses. There is no need of seeking for them; they are already at hand, and of every variety, size and shape. They are kept ready for every occasion. If one will not suit, another may be tried. Be admonished then, that a disposition to be excused is not much different from a disposition to disobey.

2. Guard against *antinomianism* on the subject of missions. There is a great tendency in these days to *say and do not*. The thrill of the missionary theme, like an exhilarating gas, is pleasant to many; but the sober and humble business of engaging in the work is not so welcome. A disposition to say much and do little is a feature of the most alarming kind. It shows an obtuseness of conscience.

3. Remember that Divine direction is better than human wisdom. We are very much inclined to argue the question, "Where can I [Pg 195] do the most good?" Be assured we can do the most good by *obeying* the Saviour: by carrying out the spirit of his last command. Let us keep *close* to that command: it is safer than to determine by

our own dark and biased reasoning, and by our very limited foresight, where we can be the most useful.

4. The nearer you live to Jesus, the more hope will there be of your coming to a right decision. There is a process of conviction and conversion before a man becomes a missionary—a serious conflict. Nothing but nearness to the Saviour will prepare a man to pass through such a conflict, and keep safely on the side of truth and duty.

5. If, after examining thoroughly and prayerfully the question of becoming a missionary, the mind waver between conflicting reasons, it will be safest to lean to the side of the greatest self-denial.

6. In selecting the place of the greatest usefulness in the wide field of the world, the best rule is, to fly to the post most likely to be deserted.

7. A kindred principle is, to do in person the more difficult and unpleasant work, and to commit the more easy and delightful to proxy. [Pg 196]

8. Remember the time is short. A few days more, and we shall meet our Saviour in the presence of a world of souls.

9. Keep in mind the conduct of our blessed Saviour, and be imbued with his spirit. Feel as he felt, and do as he did, when he beheld us in misery and in sin.

CHAPTER VIII.

TRIALS TO BE MET.

Common trials need not be named: we allude only to a few of those that are most severe. Take then first, the trial of leaving friends. The Saviour says, "He that loveth father or mother more than me is not worthy of me, and he that loveth son or daughter more than me is not worthy of me." The plain meaning is, to be Christians, our love to Christ must be supreme. Now, if it is supreme, it will show itself to be so in our conduct. There is full room, even at the present day, for a practical test of this condition of discipleship. Not only is the *spirit* of this [Pg 197] passage required, but in many cases, a *literal compliance* with the identical things named in it. This saying of our Saviour has been too much forgotten. Like some other important sayings of our Lord, it has been virtually expunged. It has been regarded as applying only to apostolic times — to times of persecution. This is a wide mistake. If all nations are to be enlightened by the use of means, there must be a practical exhibition among Christians at the present time, and in all time to come, of a love to Christ superior to the love which we owe to father, mother, son or daughter. And this love is not spoken of as a high attainment in piety, but as an indispensable condition of discipleship. The missionary enterprise presents many instances of stern necessity to test and exhibit this principle.

The occasion most familiar to the general reader, and the one best appreciated by him, is the time when missionaries go forth to the heathen. They are compelled to break away from almost every tie. The strength of attachment to all that is dear on earth, is a feeling that may be experienced, and can be imagined too, in part, but can never be de [Pg 198] scribed. There are a thousand ties, and tender ties too, that must be sundered. The loved scenes of childhood and youth, and scenes of sacred peace and pleasure that cluster about the sanctuary, the conference-room and the praying circle, must all receive a parting thought. Friends — dear friends and connections, must receive a last adieu and a lingering look. But O how keen the sensation when the last sigh, the last tear, and the last embrace is to be exchanged with father and mother, brother and sister — when all the touching associations of kindred and home are for once revived to be dismissed forever!

Imagine not that the sensibilities of missionaries are less exquisite than those of other persons. The pangs they endure are indeed alleviated by soothing considerations drawn from the Gospel; but they are, notwithstanding, deep — deeper than the looker-on may at first suppose.

There may be some persons—I have heard of such—who misrepresent the feelings and motives of missionaries in leaving their friends; who impute to them cold hearts and a bluntness of sensibility; who say that they are wanting in filial devotion, and can therefore [Pg 199] leave aged parents to droop and die: that they have a small share of fraternal affection, and that it is therefore they can break away from the embrace of brothers and sisters, and leave them in anguish and in tears. All these remarks are sometimes made, and perhaps oftener secretly indulged, than openly expressed. It is often that the missionary is not allowed to take his leave merely with a bleeding heart and a soul gushing with emotion, but is compelled to endure a keener anguish: that of knowing that the course he is taking, agonizing as it is, is imputed by some to a want of sensibility; to a destitution of the finer, tenderer, and more delicate feelings, that adorn society, and that make families lovely and happy. Here then are trials: such, however, as he must cheerfully meet for Christ's sake.

But the separation from home, with its numerous and nameless endearments, and at the risk of misrepresentation, is but the first lesson of obedience. That person whose love to Christ is so weak as to fail here on the threshold, would give but poor evidence of being prepared for similar and severer trials in prospect. The *main* occasion for exemplify [Pg 200] ing the spirit of the Saviour's words to which we have alluded, is on heathen ground, when stern necessity calls upon parents to make the best disposition in their power in regard to their own children. This is an occasion not so well understood by the Christian community as the one I have noticed. The difficulties in the way of properly training children on heathen ground are not clearly seen; neither are all the objections appreciated which attend the usual alternative, that of sending them to a Christian land. These are the occasions of trial, compared with which all other sufferings of the missionary are scarcely worthy of being named. They are trials, however, that must be met, not evaded; for the Saviour says, "He that loveth son or daughter more than me is not worthy of me." They must be cheerfully met, and counted "all joy," or we cannot claim the spirit of the first disciples.

There are those, I know, who would relieve this subject at once by proposing the celibacy of missionaries; but the argument of such persons can hardly be deemed worth considering, till they shall know a little more "what they say, and whereof they affirm." Celibacy [Pg 201] for ministers at home would be a much more proper and expedient arrangement, than for missionaries in most foreign fields. And one would think that the experience of the church, from the days of the apostles till now, had taught us enough to silence at once any such proposition, and to place it forever at rest. Were it in place for me, I could give reasons here to the heart's content: but I deem it more prudent to forbear.

The difficulties in the way of training children on heathen ground, cannot all be named; and fewer still can be justly appreciated by those who have never made the attempt. What I shall say will apply particularly to barbarous and degraded nations, such as the Sandwich Islanders once were; for it is to such nations that the missionary's eye should be specially directed.

I shall mention first, *the difficulty of keeping children from the pollutions and vices of the heathen.* Children have eyes, and among the heathen what do they see? I need only refer you to the knowledge you already possess of the naked condition, vile habits, and gross vices of a barbarous people. There is much in heathen society which cannot be described, [Pg 202] but which children must more or less witness. The state of things, in this respect, is very much improved at the Sandwich Islands; but I refer to that condition in which they once were—to that condition in which all barbarous nations are, without the light of the Gospel. Imagine then to yourself this feature of heathen society, and then repeat the inquiry, What do children see?

Again, children have ears, and they cannot be so effectually closed as to be kept from learning in some measure the language of the heathen. And if they become acquainted with the language of the heathen, what do they hear day after day? In many a pagan country they are liable to hear disputes, contentions, revilings, execration and blasphemy; but what is more, they are liable to hear in familiar, unblushing and open conversation, words and phrases which are not so much as to be named. The heathen have no forbidden words in their language. Every term is liable to be brought into public and frequent use without the least sense of impropriety.

On account of this pernicious example and vile conversation, many missionaries, where it is practicable, make walls about their [Pg 203] houses, and endeavor by strict inclosures to prevent their children from having intercourse with the natives. This can be done in some places, and to some degree, while children are young; but when they are somewhat grown up, it is preposterous to think of keeping them within inclosures. And as soon as they are out of their inclosures, there are a thousand pitfalls ready for their feet, on the right hand and on the left. How much solicitude was felt by Abraham and Isaac for their children, on account of the heathen population which surrounded them. This pernicious influence, better imagined than described, and still better seen than imagined, is one of the reasons which lead missionaries to undergo the agony of separation, and to send their children to a Christian land. This evil at the Sandwich Islands is much diminished, but not so much so as may at first glance be supposed from the progress in Christianity which has been made, and from the powerful revivals which have here been experienced.

Again it must be remarked, that children trained up on heathen shores are in danger of *contracting habits of indolence*. The heathen, as a general remark, exert themselves [Pg 204] no oftener and no longer than they feel the pressure of present want. They are far from being industrious, and farther still from anything like enterprise. Those nations that are partly civilized exhibit more or less industry, and are acquainted with some of the arts; but barbarous nations are acquainted with none of the improvements that elevate society, and exhibit a state of lounging indolence and torpid inactivity. If there be noise, it is not the rattle and whirl of business, or the hum of industry; but the noise of giddy mirth, boisterous and unmeaning laughter, or fierce and angry contention. If there be stillness, it is not the peace and quiet of well-ordered society, but the gloomy and deathlike stillness of indolence, sensuality, and beastly degradation. Now, who does not know that children are likely to be much influenced by the aspect and character of the society by which they are surrounded? Who does not know that they are likely to imbibe the spirit of the nation in which they live, whether on the one hand it be that of industry and enterprise, or on the other, that of sensual ease and torpid indolence? Let a youth be trained up in a village of intelligence, active industry and [Pg 205] stirring enterprise; let his ears be filled with the noise of business from morning till night; let him travel in stages, in steamboats and on railroads, and it will be next to impossible for him to be indolent and sluggish. But in heathen society, the whole atmosphere is entirely different; it is a choke-damp to all activity, and it falls on the senses with a benumbing and deadening influence.

But more than this, missionaries have no business in which to employ their children; and if it were possible to devise business in which to employ them, there is no one to superintend their labor. Missionaries have no time for the purpose, and no other persons, among most pagan nations, can be found who are trusty and competent. This is a stubborn fact, and stands in the way as a very great obstacle. Neither, in most cases, can the children of missionaries be kept industrious in the acquisition of knowledge. Their fathers and mothers cannot devote so much of their time to their children, as to keep their minds industriously employed in the pursuit of knowledge; and as to schools, most missions are not thus favored. Missionaries then, if they keep their children on heathen ground, [Pg 206] run the risk of seeing them grow up in habits of inactivity and indolence. This, if a risk, is a fearful one; for missionaries ardently wish their children to be useful when they themselves shall be dead. But indolence and usefulness are the opposites of each other; whereas indolence and vice are closely allied. To prevent then this deadly evil, of having their children grow up in indolent habits, is one of the strong reasons why missionaries resort to the heart-rending alternative of parting with their children, with but little probability of seeing them again this side the grave.

Again, as the state of things now is, the children of missionaries, if kept on heathen ground, can possess but *very limited advantages for mental improvement.* Their mothers cannot be depended upon to instruct them much in literature and the sciences. Under the influence of a withering atmosphere, often sick, with no help in many countries in their domestic affairs but untrusty domestics, and often with none at all, and obliged to attend to many calls from the people, or run the risk of giving offence, how can they be expected to find much time and strength for disciplining the minds of their children, and storing [Pg 207] them with useful knowledge? They may succeed in giving them an acquaintance with the branches of common education, but to carry them into the higher branches is, as a general remark, entirely out of the question. Such a task is by no means expected of a minister's wife at home, much less can it be expected of the wife of a missionary.

Neither can their fathers be depended upon to give a thorough education. Ministers at home would find it a great encroachment upon their time to spend several hours each day in instructing their own children; but they have *vastly* more leisure to do so than the foreign missionary. To instruct a class of three or four requires the same apparatus, the same preparation in the teacher, and the same number of hours each day, as would be required for a class of thirty or forty. But should a missionary devote such an amount of time and means to his own family, it must be to the neglect of other labor. The most economical, and the most efficient course by far, evidently is, to collect together a sufficient number of missionaries' children to form a school, and devote a competent number of teachers entirely to that work. [Pg 208]

But even where such schools can be enjoyed, they must be attended with many risks and privations, and be only preparatory in their nature. Those scholars, who may need a thorough education, must be still under the necessity of visiting a Christian land. It is too of great, and perhaps indispensable importance, that youth who are trained for active life should see the industry, enterprise, and intelligence of a Christian land, and so far, at least, partake of its character and imbibe its spirit.

Missionaries, then, must either suffer their children to grow up with a very limited education, or submit to the alternative sooner or later of sending them to a Christian land. But missionaries see the want of laborers in the great field of the world, and ardently desire that their children may be qualified to take part in the work. They choose therefore the present anguish of separation, bitter as it may be, that there may exist a reasonable prospect that their children, at some future day, may be eminently useful in the vineyard of the Lord.

One other difficulty I must name, and that is, that missionaries' children, if kept on hea [Pg 209] then ground, will have *no prospect of suitable employment when old enough to settle in life.* They will have no trades. To be merchants they will not have means. They will not be acquainted with agriculture, and in many countries will not be able to obtain land to cultivate. Some, who are fit for the work, may become preachers and teachers, but will not command the influence that they would if they were educated in a Christian land. Thus the prospect of suitable employment is very dark, and is a fact in the case of much weight.

These reasons and others that might be named, possess in the minds of missionaries immense force — force enough, in many instances, to induce them to tear from their embrace the dear objects of their love, and to send them over a wide ocean to the care of friends, and often to the care of strangers. They do not lead all parents to this result; for on the other hand, there are strong, very strong objections to such a course. The trial in either case is great; but it is one that must be met, not evaded. It is wise to count the cost, but it is treason to be faint-hearted; for the trial, after all, cannot weigh much in the [Pg 210] balance against the eternal interests of the dying heathen. How much worse is the condition of millions upon millions of heathen children!

The first objection in the minds of missionaries against sending their children home, is, that *such a measure seems unnatural.* That it is a violation of nature, all parents not only admit, but most deeply *feel.* God has implanted feelings in the breast of natural parents, which peculiarly fit them to take care of their own children. No other persons can precisely take their place, and feel the same interest, the same unwearied concern — the same unprovoked temper and unchangeable love through good report and through evil report. In a word, no other persons, however good and worthy, can be *natural parents.* Guardians can be found, who will feel a warm interest in those children who are bright, interesting, well-behaved and pious. But to feel properly for children that are dull, uninteresting and wayward, requires a *parent's heart.*

That this is the state of the case, is too true to be denied. For parents, then, to violate this provision of nature, is causing a [Pg 211] sword to pierce through their own bosoms, and the bosoms of their children: to do it without sufficient reasons, is to act at variance

108

with the God who made them. In the feelings implanted in the breasts of parents towards their children, God has established a general rule: has made known his will, his law, and indelibly inscribed it on the parent's heart. Missionaries must be able to plead an *exception* to this general law, or they will be found to be opposing the will of their Maker. That the very strong reasons they can urge really justify an exception, is plain to the minds of many, but not to the minds of all.

Another objection arises from the command binding upon parents to train up their children in the nurture and admonition of the Lord. It is clear to the minds of some missionaries, that the spirit of this and similar commands is complied with when they make provision, according to the best of their judgment, for the religious education of their children. By others it is thought, that these explicit commands of God cannot be obeyed by any arrangement which commits the work to proxy; that there is risk in committing the work to others; that fully to obey God, parents, if not [Pg 212] removed by death, must *in person* pray with their children and instruct them in the truths of the Gospel; and that they must do this, not only through the period of childhood, but also through the season of youth, or till their children are old enough to think and act for themselves. It is admitted by all, that it is *desirable* that parents should do this interesting and responsible work in person. No one else can do it with the feeling and unction natural to parents. All not only admit this to be true, but *feel* it, too, to the very centre of their souls. But some think that it is not only very desirable, but altogether indispensable — that any other course is an unwarrantable substitution of human wisdom for the explicit direction of the all-wise God. The reader must judge whether this position is tenable or not.

There is another objection: If missionaries' children are sent home, then one very important *influence of a missionary's family upon the heathen* is in a great measure lost. Among the heathen, the family constitution is in ruins. The state of society is almost a perfect chaos. It is of immense importance, therefore, not only to inculcate the principles [Pg 213] of domestic peace, but actually to bring before their eyes living examples of well-ordered and happy families. They need to see, not only young children well governed, but also the mutual interchanges of love, affection and duty, between young people and their aged parents. But this they cannot see if children are sent home. A missionary's family, who sends his older children home, and keeps with him only those that are quite young, is not like a tree adorned with its natural and well-proportioned branches, but presents the aspect of a tree closely trimmed, and with only a few twigs left at the very top. And when all his children are sent away, his family presents the aspect of a trunk without branch, shoot, twig or foliage, standing alone in an open field. This is unnatural, blighting to much of the comfort and cheerfulness of the parental abode, and is not the example which it is desirable to hold up before the eyes of the heathen. One important reason, then, why a missionary should have a family, is lost in sending his children home.

I mention as another objection, the dangerous influence to which children are more or less exposed on a *long voyage at sea*. From [Pg 214] some of the missionary fields, the voyage must be five, six, or seven months. I speak not of what are called the dangers of the deep, or the hardships of a sea life for six or seven months. These are of little account. The danger of which I speak is, the pernicious influence to which for that length of time they are exposed. This is an objection which, though not of sufficient weight in itself to determine one's course, may yet come in as an item in making up the account.

On the supposition that children are sent, they go of course without their parents. In some cases the protector to whom they are to be intrusted may not be altogether such as could be desired. Even in case a parent accompanies the children, he will find it a great task to keep them from many pernicious influences during a long voyage. In very many ships they will hear more or less profane, low, vulgar and infamous language, both in conversation and in song. They will see exhibitions of anger, impatience, fretfulness, boisterous laughter and giddy mirth. They will see the holy Sabbath made a day of business, or at best a day of lounging and idleness. They will be likely on the one hand to receive [Pg 215] such caresses as to make them vain and self-important; or, on the other hand, to be so treated as to chafe their tempers and injure their dispositions. In short, for six or seven months, they must be thrown into a strange family; into a family confined to the narrow limits of a ship's cabin and deck;

into a family over which the parent of the children has no control; into a family, too, composed of the variety of character and disposition of those who sail on the ocean. Thus circumstanced, children inevitably suffer much, even under the vigilant eye of a parent, and still more would they suffer under any eye less careful and attentive. This moral danger to which children are exposed at sea, though not an objection of the strongest kind, is yet an item worthy of being noticed. Missionaries think of it when sending away their children, and dread it far more than tempests and tornadoes.

Another objection is, that *no adequate provision is made for the support and education of missionaries' children*, if sent to a Christian land. The provision that is made by the American Board of Commissioners is $60 a year for a boy till he is eighteen years of age, [Pg 216] and $50 a year for a girl during the same period. Now, every one sees that this is a sum scarcely sufficient to furnish them with food and clothing, without provision for sickness or means of education. It may be said, that they must be thrown much upon the spontaneous charities of Christians and of friends. But such a dependence must be uncertain, especially as few Christians appreciate the reasons and feelings of missionaries in sending home their children. Who of my readers in Christian lands would be willing to throw his own child on such a precarious subsistence?

But the strongest objection, in my opinion is this: *If no other course can be adopted than that of sending the children home, it is to be feared that the number of missionaries will never be so increased as to afford a rational prospect of the world's conversion.* While the plan of sending children home is cherished, it will seem so incompatible with a large number of laborers, that it will tend to perpetuate the destructive notion, that the nations are to be saved by the labors of merely a few hundred men. But if means are to be employed in any measure commensurate with the end [Pg 217] in view, a few men cannot put forth the instrumentality needed to elevate all nations. To commit the work to a few is in truth to relinquish it. If, then, the measure of sending children home should tend in the least to favor this destructive notion, it must, if possible, be avoided. This tendency is disastrous; and is, of course, an objection of immense force.

It is clear that there are, on the one hand, very strong reasons for sending children home, and on the other hand, very strong objections to such a course. Missionaries, then, are reduced to a very trying dilemma. Whichever course they choose, it is equally distressing. Whichever way they turn, they find enough to rend their hearts with anguish. There are two cups, mixed indeed with different ingredients, but equally bitter, one of which they must drink. Their only comfort is to look upward, pour their sorrows into the ear of God, and cast their cares on him who careth for them. This is a trial, the sting of which cannot be appreciated except by those who have felt it. It is by far the greatest trial of the missionary, and probably greater than all his other trials combined. [Pg 218] The pain of leaving one's kindred and country is nothing compared with it.

But if the cup be of such a mixture, can there be found those whose hearts are so insensible as to throw in other ingredients to make the draught more bitter? If missionaries keep their children, and ask for the requisite means of education, shall they be called extravagant? If they send them home, shall they be regarded as possessing but a small share of natural affection?

Here, then, are trials; but however great, they are to be met, not evaded—met by the churches, met by missionaries; and however severe and agonizing such trials, they are nothing in the balance against the dying condition of the heathen. The situation of our children, trying as it is, is unspeakably better than that of three hundred millions of heathen children and youth. The Saviour commands—the world is dying—and he that loveth son or daughter more than Christ is not worthy of him.

The inquiry is worth notice, Whether the situation of missionaries cannot be so altered as to change very materially the state of the [Pg 219] question, in regard to their children? Would not such a change be effected by the going forth of laymen in great numbers, and of all the useful professions, arts and employments, so as to form little circles here and there over the earth?

A great part of the heathen world is open for such classes of men. Appeals for such men have been sent from Africa, Asia Minor, Siam, the Sandwich Islands, and in short from almost every mission. They would of course labor under greater or less disadvantages; but these disadvantages should only have the effect to call forth the more energy, patience and perseverance.

But it will be asked, How would the going forth of such classes of men better the condition of missionaries' children?

1. They would afford society, form a public sentiment, and thus serve in a measure to keep children from the influence of a heathen population. It is already found on heathen ground, that where there are several families of missionaries, the children form a society among themselves; but where there is but one family, the children are more inclined to seek society among the degraded objects about them. [Pg 220]

2. Again, if men of various useful employments should be located with the missionary, there would be held up before the children examples of Christian industry and enterprise; whereas, in their present isolated condition, the children suffer from an atmosphere of indolence and stagnation.

3. The going forth of such men to introduce the different arts and occupations, would afford suitable employment for the children and youth of missionaries, and furnish them to some extent with permanent situations in mature life.

4. If there were such little circles of laymen as we suppose, they would have at whatever sacrifice, as the Pilgrims of New England did, institutions of learning among themselves, where children and youth might receive a suitable education.

Unless some arrangement of this kind can be made, the trials of missionaries must remain unrelieved and unmitigated. And even with such an arrangement, the trial would be only in part removed. Even then the children of foreign laborers would by no means receive all the advantages of a Christian land, neither would they be shielded from all the evils of a [Pg 221] heathen community. But it is worthy of thought, whether by such an arrangement they would not be so far shielded, and possess advantages to such an amount, as to change the preponderance of argument.

Then, in addition to this or some similar arrangement, should not Christians *be more liberal in affording means and facilities for education, and expect of missionaries to devote to their children more of their time?*

I have now brought before your minds the greatest of all missionary trials; and yet I urge many of you, ministers and laymen, and urge you considerately and solemnly too, to enter the work. I have not hesitated to state freely the whole difficulty, for I am in no wise unwilling that you should count the cost. And I would say with Gideon, "Whosoever is fearful and afraid, let him return and depart early." God desires no faint-hearted men in his service. He desires men that shrink from no self-denial for his sake. For after their trials are over—and they will be but short[1]—he wishes to crown them with glory, and place them at his own right hand as partners [Pg 222] of his throne. He will place no unbelieving, faint-hearted men there. He will place none there who are not "worthy of him." And remember that he said, "He that loveth son or daughter more than me, is not worthy of me."

[1: The author, soon after writing this appeal, was called to enter into the joy of his Lord.]

In looking at the embarrassment of missionaries in regard to their children, a thought something like this is apt to arise: missionaries are by profession a class of self-denying persons, and this trial is only in consistency with the life they have chosen. Now, where in the Bible do you find, that a spirit of self-denial and of consecration is enjoined peculiarly upon missionaries more than upon others? Where do you find it intimated, that a missionary spirit is a thing superadded to Christian character? An entire consecration of our children to Christ is not a test of missionary spirit, but a test of discipleship. Not the missionary, but "*He*, that loveth son or daughter more than me, is not worthy of me."

The spirit of this injunction requires *all* parents to train up their children in that way in which they may be of the greatest service [Pg 223] to Christ; and not only to be willing—that would be but a small measure of Christian feeling—but earnestly and constantly to pray, that they may be employed in that part of his vineyard, and in that kind of work, where they can be instrumental of the most good, even though it be on some distant shore, teaching the alphabet to the ignorant and degraded.

But is this the spirit which prevails in the churches? I have seen it stated that, of twenty or more young men in a theological institution, who were at the same time agitating the question of their duty to become missionaries, *all but two were discouraged by their parents, and these two were the sons of widows.* Many other facts of a similar kind might be added, if it were best to name them. Many parents give their children to the Lord when young, and talk of locating them on the shores of Japan, or New Guinea; but the very manner of educating them—in softness, delicacy and helplessness—shows at once the inefficacy of such a profession. Many parents are quite ready to consecrate their children before they become pious. "O, if the Saviour would only convert my child, I would readily [Pg 224] yield him to go to any part of the world, and to perform any service for which he might be fitted." The child becomes a Christian, and proposes to go to the heathen. The parents cling, dissuade, and throw every consideration in the way to keep him at home.

At the judgment day, if I mistake not, we shall see a great deal of our conduct in a different light from what we do now.

The spirit of the Gospel is a spirit of self-denial for the sake of Christ. The Saviour is worthy of our highest love, and no earthly attachment can be allowed to come in competition with the supreme affection which we owe to him. This love to Christ must be manifested by obeying his commandments. To yield strict obedience to Christ in this world, disordered and confused by sin, it is frequently necessary to sunder some of the tenderest ties on earth. Keen as is the sensation, it must be endured. A child must not cling unduly to a parent, nor a parent to a child, but each cling with more ardent feelings and firmer grasp to Jesus Christ and his cause. This world is not our rest. Neither is it a place to give much indulgence to many of the fond affections of the soul. There is no time [Pg 225] for it. We live in a world of sin—a confused, disordered and chaotic world—in a revolted territory, among a crowd of sinners dying an eternal death. The main point then is, to save our own souls and the souls of as many as possible of our fellow men, before the grave shall close upon us. The indulgence of many of our tenderer feelings of love and fondness must be postponed to a more peaceful abode. While in a world of dying souls, self-denial and laborious effort are most in place. Parental and filial affection should be deep and ardent indeed, but under the control of judgment. Love to Christ and to souls must predominate and govern our conduct.